AF411207

Julie Graham and Maria Friedrich
Exhibition Guest Co-curators

Catalogue Essay by Francesco Bonami

Exhibition and catalogue funded in part by
the Aspen Art Museum National Council, Judith F. Heisley, General Service Foundation,
The Lauder Foundation — Leonard and Evelyn Lauder Fund,
Melva Bucksbaum, Robert Lehrman, Jan and Ronald K. Greenberg

JENNIFER BARTLETT

VIJA CELMINS

JOSEPH CORNELL

MARY CORSE

JEAN DUBUFFET

KATHARINA FRITSCH

ANDY GOLDSWORTHY

REBECCA HORN

RONI HORN

ANISH KAPOOR

WILLIAM KENTRIDGE

YVES KLEIN

KOO JEONG-A

WOLFGANG LAIB

JULIAN LETHBRIDGE

MAYA LIN

RICHARD LONG

SUZANNE MCCLELLAND

ANA MENDIETA

ELIZABETH MURRAY

DAVID NASH

RIVANE NEUENSCHWANDER

CORNELIA PARKER

MARK ROTHKO

NANCY RUBINS

EDWARD RUSCHA

ANTONI TAPIÈS

JUAN USLÉ

ANDY WARHOL

MEG WEBSTER

JACKIE WINSOR

YUKINORI YANAGI

DAISY YOUNGBLOOD

The Aspen Art Museum
25 February – 11 April 1999

For
Robin Graham
and
Michael McTwigan

POWDER

Copyright ©1999
Aspen Art Museum
590 North Mill Street
Aspen, Colorado 81611
970-925-8050

All rights reserved.

Catalogue design
Salsgiver Coveney Associates Inc.

Printed by
Pacific Rim International
Hong Kong

Library of Congress
Catalogue Card Number
98-74829

ISBN 0-934324-25-5

Ace Gallery
Chase Manhattan Collection
Paula Cooper Gallery
Peggy and Dick Danziger
Zoe and Joel Dictrow
Gary and JoAnn Fink
Stephen Friedman Gallery
The Frith Street Gallery
Galerie Lelong
Gagosian Gallery
Barbara Gladstone Gallery
Marian Goodman Gallery
The Stephen Hahn Family Collection
Mr. and Mrs. James R. Hedges IV Collection
Paul Kasmin Gallery
Koo Jeong-a
Robert Lehrman Collection
Julian Lethbridge
Maya Lin
Amy and Richard Lipton
Matthew Marks Gallery
The Nancy and Bob Magoon Collection
David and Renee McKee
David Nash
National Gallery of Art, Washington
Rivane Neuenschwander
Cornelia Parker
Private collection
Christopher Rothko
Martin Sklar
Sperone Westwater Gallery
Andy Warhol Foundation for the Visual Arts, Inc.
Weaver Collection
Meg Webster
PaceWildenstein Gallery

ASPEN ART MUSEUM

NATIONAL COUNCIL

Jan & Ronald K. Greenberg,
Co-Chairs
Sylvia & Richard Kaufman,
Vice-Chairs

Joan Anderman
Diane Anderson
Peggy & Charles E. Balbach
Harley Baldwin & Richard Edwards
Anne Bass
Barbara & Bruce Berger
Marie & Robert Bergman
Jill & Jay Bernstein
Barbara S. Bluhm
Kay & Matt Bucksbaum
Mary Bucksbaum
Melva Bucksbaum
Dale Coudert
Mary H. Dayton
Frannie Dittmer
Tom Dittmer
Holly & David Dreman
Nanette & Jerry Finger
Kathryn Fleck
Merrill Ford & General Robert Taylor
Rosemary & Richard Furman
Mary Jane Garth
Gideon Gartner
Linda & Bob Gersh
Audrey & Arthur Greenberg
Lundy & Jim Hedges

Lita & Morton Heller
Phyllis Hojel
Lorry & Tom Hubbard
Ann & Edward R. Hudson, Jr.
Holly Hunt
Jane & Gerald Katcher
Susan & Bruce Konheim
Pamela & Richard Kramlich
Toby Devan Lewis
Marilyn & Donn Lipton
Cornelia & Meredith Long
Nancy & Robert Magoon
Marlene & Frederic V. Malek
Nancy & Peter Meinig
Gail & J. Alec Merriam
Gael Neeson & Stefan T. Edlis
Judith Neisser
Ann & William Nitze
Linda Pace & Laurence Miller
Pat & Manny Papper
Julia & Waring Partridge
Pixie & James J. Reiss, Jr.
Lynda & Stewart Resnick
Danner & Arno D. Schefler
June & Paul Schorr
Barbara & Robert Shook
Bren & Melvin Simon
Shirley & Albert Small
Julie & Barry Smooke
Gay & William T. Solomon
Ginny Williams
Ruth & Herb Winter

BOARD OF TRUSTEES

Susan Marx, *President*
Nancy Magoon,
Vice President for Development
Joyce Gruenberg, *Co-Treasurer*
Bob Sullivan, *Co-Treasurer*
Nancy Epstein, *Secretary*
Randy Beier
Barbara Broeder
Elaine Cahn
Laurie Crown
Charles Cunniffe
Holly Dreman
Richard Edwards
Jill Fink
Ana Goldberg
Jane Jellinek
Tony Mazza
Dick Osur
Mike Otte
Ed Roth
John Sarpa
Tom Sharkey
Betty Weiss
Lorrie Winnerman
Jan & Ronald K.Greenberg,
National Council Representatives
Arthur C. Daily, Esq.,
of counsel

MUSEUM STAFF

Suzanne Farver, *Executive Director*
Mary Ann Igna, *Associate Director*
Susan Claire Burston,
Director of Development
Dara Coder, *Accountant*
Laura Curry, *Art Trips*
Dana Geraghty, *Preparator/Designer*
Meggan Bly Humphrey,
Director of Public Relations
Gaylen Marsh, *Membership*
Cathleen Murphy, *Registrar*
Janel Stewart, *Receptionist/Bookshop*

Suzanne Farver
Executive Director, Aspen Art Museum

The production of the POWDER exhibition has been a significant act of team-
work and cooperation on many fronts. I would first like to thank Julie Augur
for planting the idea of this show into our heads and for suggesting two gifted
curators to execute it. Without the leadership of Julie Graham and Maria
Friedrich the idea would have remained just that, an idea. But because of
Julie's unfailing enthusiasm and Maria's centered energy, we turned a dream
into reality. It has been a joy to work with them both, and this catalogue is a
great testament to their talents and to that of Karen Salsgiver, its designer.

Financial support was a major factor in ensuring a quality exhibition, and the
leadership and commitment of the Aspen Art Museum National Council was a
vital force in the decision to go ahead. As the show and catalogue came into
focus and we knew we would need additional funding, other wonderful Museum
friends stepped up to help. Our sincere thanks to the Aspen Art Museum
National Council, Judith F. Heisley, General Service Foundation, The Lauder
Foundation — Leonard and Evelyn Lauder Fund, Melva Bucksbaum, Robert
Lehrman, Jan and Ronald K. Greenberg, and to other generous donors whose
contributions came in after press deadline.

Thanks, too, to our wonderful Board of Trustees, who gave us the backing
and support to undertake this exhibition. It was a big step for us, and their
confidence in our staff is greatly appreciated.

Several staff members worked long hours to make everything go smoothly.
I'd like to especially thank associate director Mary Ann Igna, exhibition designer
Dana Geraghty, and registrar Cathleen Murphy. As usual, it's been a pleasure
to work with you all.

December 1998

Acknowledgments

Julie Graham and Maria Friedrich
Exhibition Guest Co-curators

First and foremost, we would like to thank each of the artists for their profound contribution.

Exhibitions represent the collective and analytical ideas of a moment or an age, and without documentation can become lost in the history of time. Critical and timely support to produce the catalogue and underwrite the cost of this exhibition was graciously provided, and we are very grateful.

We would like to thank the lenders who agreed to participate in the exhibition and whose trust allowed us to bring their artworks to the Aspen Art Museum. We feel indebted to the following individuals for their cooperation and patience offered: Amy and Richard Lipton, Gary and JoAnn Fink, Mr. and Mrs. James R. Hedges IV, Nancy and Bob Magoon, David and Renee McKee, John Weaver, Peggy and Dick Danziger, Robert Lehrman, Zoe and Joel Dictrow, Christopher Rothko and Martin Sklar.

Many individuals from a network of international galleries, museums, private foundations and corporate collections were especially helpful and we are grateful to each of them. Jeffrey Weiss, Associate Curator of 20th-Century Art, and Nancy Stanfield, Museum Specialist in the Department of Imaging and Visual Services, of the National Gallery of Art, Washington; Susan Davidson, Associate Curator and Geraldine Aramanda, Rights and Reproductions Coordinator of the Menil Collection, Houston; Achim Moeller of Achim Moeller Fine Art, Ltd.; Charlotta Kotik, Curator of Contemporary Art, Brooklyn Museum of Art; Madeleine Taylor of ACE Gallery, New York; Barbara Gladstone, Ivy Shapiro, and Rainald Schumacher of Barbara Gladstone Gallery, New York; Manuel Gonzalez and Patty Hinsdale of Chase Manhattan Collection; David Lieber of Sperone Westwater Gallery, New York; Christopher Rothko; Marion Kahan of the Kate Rothko Prizel and Christopher Rothko Collections; Douglas Baxter, Susan Dunne and Kate Zamet of PaceWildenstein Gallery, New York; Paula Cooper, Steve Henry, Ona Nowina-Sapinski and Charlyne Maddox of Paula Cooper Gallery, New York; Bob Monk of Gagosian Gallery, New York; Mary Sabbatino and Cécile Panzieri of Galerie Lelong, New York; Jill Sussman and Jeannie Freilich-Sondik of Marian Goodman Gallery, New York; Rose Lord of Frith Street Gallery, London; the Estate of Ana Mendieta; Paul Kasmin of Paul Kasmin Gallery, New York; Renee McKee of McKee Gallery, New York; Andrew Leslie of Matthew Marks Gallery, New York; John Cheim, Howard Read and Kristin Edwards of Cheim Read Gallery, New York; Vincent Fremont of Vincent Fremont Enterprises, Inc.; Tim Hunt and Claudia Defendi of The Andy Warhol Foundation; Michael Hue-Williams of Michael Hue-Williams Fine Art Ltd., London; Jimmy Corcoran and Tracy Lew of Corcoran Gallery, Los Angeles; Peter Blum, Arthur Solway of BlumArts; Jennifer Vorbach of C & M Arts, New York; Ronnie Greenberg of Greenberg Van Doren Gallery, St. Louis; Paul Gray of Richard Gray Gallery, New York/Chicago; Allan, Clare and Claudia Stone of the Allan Stone Gallery; Sherry Shieh of the Maya Lin Studio; Thea Westreich Art Advisory Services; the Jennifer Bartlett Studio; Patricia Kohl of the Stephen Friedman Gallery, London; Mary Dean of the Edward Ruscha Studio; and Linda Givon of the Goodman Gallery, Johannesburg, South Africa.

Within the Aspen Art Museum, we would like to acknowledge Suzanne Farver, Executive Director, and Mary Ann Igna, Associate Director for their pivotal support; Registrar Cath Murphy, who administered many complex arrangements for the safe arrival of all artworks; Meggan Bly Humphrey, Public Relations Director; Dana Geraghty, Exhibition and Graphic Designer for her exquisite installation concept and able crew; to Frank Yantorno, Preparator, for his sensitive handling of all art works; to Dara Coder, Accountant, for her patience and accuracy. The production of this elegant catalogue would not have been possible without the inspiration, direction and design from Karen Salsgiver; Alexis Toriello's typing; and Michael McTwigan's discerning copy editing and support.

Francesco Bonami deserves special recognition for his illuminating essay written between his international guest critic activities.

We thank and offer special recognition to Paula Cooper, Bob Monk, Manuel Gonzalez, Mary Sabbatino, Cécile Panzieri, Douglas Baxter, Renee McKee, Carol Marcuso Ungaro and Margaret Watherston. We are indebted for their professional and collegial generosity. To Jai Imbrey, for her wisdom and impeccable translations in French; to Lindsay Shea for her support; Karen McCready and Victoria Munroe for their sage advice; to Gretchen Berggruen and Phillip Bruno for their contributions.

Finally, it is to Julie Augur, Suzanne Farver and Mary Ann Igna that we owe our deep thanks for extending the initial invitation to us to co-curate this exhibition.

For decades, biologists have known that the body's
mortality is mirrored on the cellular level by an
immutable rule called the Hayflick Limit.
—   Nicholas Wade,
     The New York Times/Science Times,
     November 15, 1998.

Do we really want to be immortal?

I mean to live forever, to challenge the gods, to piss them
off, to be struck by thunder, to get up again and go home
day after day, for all eternity, to the same postman, the same
neighbor, the same cat, dog or goldfish, the same menus
under the door, the same Sunday *Times,* the same people
writing reviews and the same people reading them, with no
obituary page, no end, never?

Art's future depends upon our answer and upon the
possibility that some day we will really be immortal. Some
people, such as Dr. Michael West of Geron and Advanced
Cell Technology, are hard at work on this project, and one
day Dr. Hayflick's limit will be overcome and funerary
homes will have to close and cemeteries will be converted
into parking lots. No more flowers, memories, useless
sorrows or wasted tears. If people had been created to last
forever we would still have Duchamp among us, not doing
"readymades" any longer but a series of pedantic pranks.
Pollock, even if limping after his car crash, would have
probably entered an insignificant but even more lucrative
figurative revival. Picasso would be (hopefully) flirting with
my daughter; Eva Hesse would be working on an expensive
show for the Prada Foundation; and Ana Mendieta would one
day become the minister of culture in a democratic Cuba.

Yet we die, dramatically and tragically, some of us too soon,
some of us too late. So art remains our one chance of
attaining immortality — and as we create we fool time, we
stretch our minds beyond the boundaries of our bodies
and for a moment, successfully or not, we try to be happy.
Mortality and not fantasy is what produces the energy in
each creative act. The anxiety of the end, a fear of the last
threshold, is what makes a few of us artists. Out of fear we
produce images, words, music, architecture — all of this
interesting enough to become the backbone of human
history, the milestone of our slow rolling towards the end.

POWDER is an exhibition conceived around that instant when
the artist attacks my, his or her own anxiety and
produces enough adrenaline to transform fear into desire,
desire into a gesture, and a gesture into what we are
accustomed to calling a "work of art," one of those apparently
insignificant objects that have the power to defeat time,
to postpone the world's end after the last image.

In the Italian language powder and dust are contained in
one word, *polvere. Polvere* defines two things at the same
time: the way Time visualizes its accumulation and the
substance produced by the human hand in order to
transform any material into its pure essence, into its last
stage before its final disappearance. Cremation is, after all,
the ultimate attempt to spare the body a series of useless
transmutations, transforming it into its purest and
original state — powder, dust, ashes.

As an exhibition, POWDER forms its narrative knot around
the idea of accumulation, but following a line of constant
transformation of the concept, leaving the ideas behind each
work to rot. Yet POWDER is not an exhibition about the
sublime, it's not the attempt to frame a delusional idea of
perfection within the conventions of the museum's walls.
POWDER expresses, through the selection of the artists, both
the human desire to believe in the transubstantiation of each
substance to a divine state and also the violence that any
material undergoes in order to became symbolic, timeless.

None of the artists in the show are escaping the "now,"
rather they are positioning their actions as works in a
painful state of longing. Producing within the "now" forces
them to bind themselves to a kind of pulverized syntax or
language that can either be dispersed through the present's
woven net, which is formed by the past where each work
defines its limits, or thrown into the future where objects
and visions may be either forgotten or celebrated. In a
suspended state between oblivion and glory, each work of
art functions momentarily, successfully, as a fragment
of some sort of sacred scripture which contains in its
essence its own translation, a system of communication
that might spread across the limitations of language.

We do not have to experience the claustrophobia of
South African reality to confront William Kentridge's
subliminal approach to violence. Within the landscape
they represent, his drawings contain a tragedy written in
invisible ink. Kentridge diffuses the memories that stones,
trees and sky carry inside of them through the monochrome
atmosphere of his images. These drawings are one of the
many centers of POWDER, but definitely the point where fear
and desire converge, producing a short-circuit. Wolfgang
Laib's yellow pollen stands opposite to Kentridge's vision.
The yellow heap of precious dust appears as the vanishing
point of a century through which two civilizations —
west and east — are trying to pass together, simultaneously,
defining their similarities and their differences.

One century — the 20th — is dramatically marked by a
sense of difference. It's a century severed between races
and religions, economic systems and political ideals.
The powder of Hiroshima and the ashes of the Holocaust
still cover the shelves of the library of progress. It is possibly
in the mechanical, back-and-forth movement of regret and
denial that Rebecca Horn's work achieves its magical
momentum. And guilt is a soft, gray surface quite similar
to Julian Lethbridge's canvases. His marks are uncertain yet
automatic wounds over the aesthetic process. His paintings
mirror the surface of history like a dried-up river of thought
where many subsidiaries create an exploded vision.

Contemporary culture is, in fact, a river of images
transformed into a network of subsidiaries. The model,
the original, the main path to the ocean disappears or is
diverted into an obscure global lagoon. Anish Kapoor
struggles to surface upon the quicksand of modernism,
following the directions of two cultures toward one cardinal
point. His forms, one next to another, form an interrupted
dialogue between two forms of logic. A conversation between
the logic of materiality and the logic of a tradition whose
faith is based on the ephemeral.

The core of POWDER is maybe the core of this very
conversation, where the artists all talk about the same
doubts and troubles but each from a slightly different
perspective. Troubles and doubts about existence are
here the cornerstones of any artistic production.
The viewer and the author both wonder about a possible
solution through idiosyncratic views.

So much of Vija Celmins' work addresses the void of
the environment that Ed Ruscha's gunpowder drawings
appear as the answer to a reality clogged with empty icons.
Both artists present a faded relationship to the world,
conceptualizing the simplest way to represent it, drawings and
paintings. Balancing the concrete aspects of representation
with the sublime necessity of describing a conflicted
spiritual state is the expressive focus of Katharina Fritsch's
sculptural research. The object is invaded with mnemonic
energy. In Fritsch's work, remembering and dreaming
overlap, blurring the contours of fears and nightmares.
Her hyper-reality crosses the border of virtual experience,
landing in a world that's neither failed nor perfect but
suspended in a limbo of looming artificiality.

Artificial life is also an intriguing concept that offers us
immortality while pick-pocketing our spirituality. But art
in general is a similarly odd practice of envisioning spiritual
ideas through artificial artifacts. Any artwork is artificial
because it is extracted from the natural process of thinking
and exposed to the conceptual act of looking. Looking at
an artwork means experiencing the artificial manifestation
of an idea. What we actually look at is the dust of thoughts,
the powder of illumination. Most of the artists in this show
continually reveal the dramatic act of creating this chasm
between the molecules of the body and its true substance
and origin, dust.

All of Anselm Kiefer's work is excavated from the dust of
memory. His paintings are tunnels below the ground of
awareness, in a realm where mythology and horror
continuously exchange roles to produce the tragedy of a
revolving misunderstanding. Mortality is the soil where
Kiefer's work fights the weeds of history. A soil where
Maya Lin's vanishing point aspired to heal the furrows
opened by recent historical misconduct. Or the soil that
makes the ground that Richard Long crosses over and over
in order to cope with a lost sense of time, pulverized by a
present craving for immediate information, avoiding the
burden of slow-cooking content.

For Ana Mendieta, on the other hand, the earth was a
place in which to hide a different identity, mixing with
elements that once generated freedom and independence.
Her body as a tombstone for her spirit and her stream of
thoughts, fragmented by a controversial reality. A reality
where Joseph Cornell, Mark Rothko and Andy Warhol
established the power of mere surface, the stage, the
primordial screen from which reality is kept afar in order
to maintain their fantasy in one simple and safe dimension.
A veil, a membrane upon which to project the simplicity
of the instant, the superficiality of the gaze, in order to
maintain the doubt of vision.

Still, vision is something that can be suddenly clouded or
fogged over and, as in Borges' experience, it abandons bodies
and objects to a state of perpetual dream, a continuous
effort to recover through words the materiality of existence.
We then survive by the power of fragrances, different smells
and odors, by the power of the tactile, no longer navigating
in a realm of images but in a maze of textures.

Meg Webster's work functions exactly on this borderline
between textures, grains, smell and shapes. Fictional borders
are raised in front of our senses or, as in Yukinori Yanagi's
ants' flags, small creatures make a Sisyphean effort to
rearrange a world destined to crumble. In a humorous way
— even if the insects are dead-serious — Yanagi tells us of a
possible world where borders becomes meaningless, where
we all strive to rearrange geography according to our private
fantasy of a world that will never exist because it's made of
concrete arteries and rocky mountains and the only powder
left is that of migrations, pogroms and mass tourism. Minor
debris moved swiftly by imploding revolutions.

We cross a moment in history where the immensity of
time is inconsiderate of our 24-inch dimension. The screen
gets dusty day after day, pushing the future up against the
static crystals of a monitor. Yet we know that our footprints
are resting in the past.

There might be no safety net waiting for the next somersault
under this thin layer of powder. Every work of art in this
exhibition floats on top of this *polvere,* they appear as different
domes of different cathedrals, worshipping different religions
in the ultimate hope that our faith will deliver salvation.

In the dark, the white mountains of aspirin by Koo Jeong-a,
the hope of a continuous dawn is projected. We wish that the
light would remain suspended in that eternal state of rising,
never to rise. That horizon behind the "Oslo" skyline is
the Hayflick Limit of contemporary culture. We know that
sooner or later this limit could be surpassed and the light
pushed behind the white mountains, higher into the endless
realm of immortality. Yet, we wish for that moment to be
delayed because the mystery of an incipient end is always
better than the familiarity of the clearest beginning.

©Francesco Bonami New York 1998

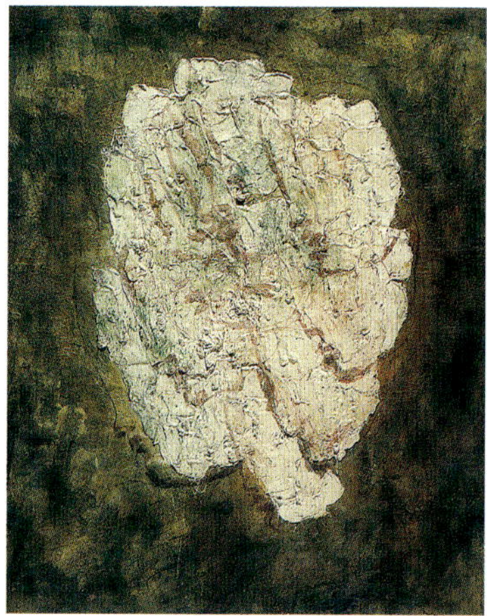

Jean Fautrier
Oradour-sur-Glane 1945
oil, waterbased paint and flecked dry pigment
on paper, mounted on canvas
57⅛" x 44⅜"
The Menil Collection, Houston, Texas

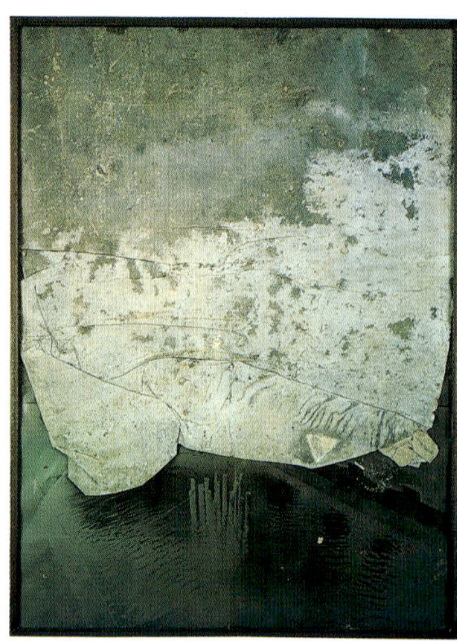

Anselm Kiefer
Brennstabe 1987-89
mixed media in steel frame
58⅛" x 39⅜"
Private collection, Greenberg Van Doren
Gallery, St. Louis, Missouri

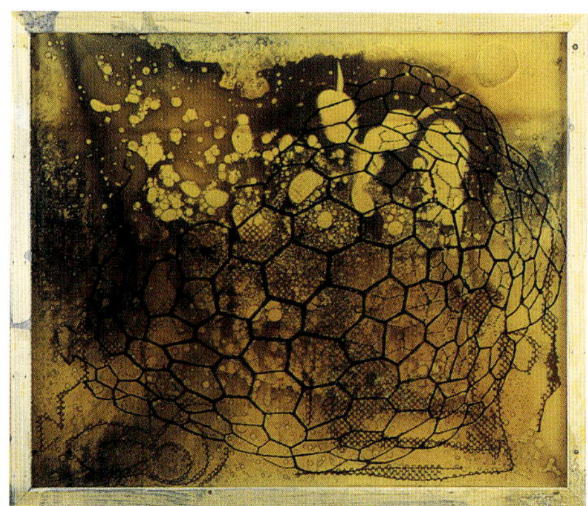

Sigmar Polke
There Is Nothing More Real than Pictures
You Can't Get Out of Your Mind 1998
mixed media on fabric
51¼" x 59"
Private collection,
Courtesy Michael Werner Gallery,
New York and Cologne

Powder, fine granules, mist, breath, the essence…human beings have been seeking the elemental building blocks of life since we gained consciousness. Bards have speculated that life arose from dust — and just as eloquently they conjure a return to it. To surmise that the universe could be found in a "mote of dust" was first proposed in 59 BC by Lucretius, the Latin author of the epic poem, "On the Nature of Things."

The urge to get at the most fundamental nature of being is a global phenomenon expressed in the ceremonial arts of the aborigines of Australia, the monks of Tibet, the Yoruba of Africa and the Navajo of the American Southwest. All used powder — sand, dirt and mineral pigments — to evoke the elemental forces or spirits. Believed to possess all the healing and destructive powers of their gods, these magical powders were meant not only to visually inspire, but also to literally enliven those who touched them. Navajo suffering from illness sat upon the sand painting to be healed. Made for a religious, rather than a secular purpose, these powder paintings in sand were deliberately impermanent. Once their magic had been invoked, their purpose was fulfilled. The artist/shaman who labored for hours to gather the dust and pigments now let it all scatter to the winds again, invoking a compassionate, respectful and clear acceptance of the cycle of birth and death.

Applying pigment to our own bodies is an equally ancient means by which mineral or vegetable powder is used to imbue its wearer with spiritual and physical power. Ritual use included body decoration to ensure a warrior's victory in battle or the hunter's ability to capture his prey. Among the cosmetic powders believed to have such power are: dried, powdered blood to evoke the spirit of the hunted; pulverized precious stones to confer the power of the gods; ground seeds to symbolize fertility; ashes to conjure the deceased. Thespis, the Greek poet who invented tragedy in the 6th century BC, may have also been the first to smear his face with white lead and red cinnabar to better portray a character. In our time, we use powdered cosmetics to enhance beauty, sex appeal or confer status, serving similar, if more secular, purposes.

Like most farsighted artists of modern times, many of the artists in POWDER are trying to capture the elusive spirit of a place or time, heal the schism between art and spirit or exorcise the presence of sinister powers, while forging a new artistic vocabulary.

The redefinition of art's purpose and meaning accelerated in the early decades of this century. The First World War brought people all over the world to the brink of global conflagration. Never before had mankind witnessed destruction on this scale. Meanwhile, the shocking revelations of Freud exposed a new perspective on the human psyche, as Einstein's Theory of Relativity seemed to overthrow entrenched concepts of space and time. In the midst of such seeming chaos, some artists decried all established artistic conventions and embraced the irrational and the accidental. Called Dada, this movement would give impetus to Surrealism, inform Abstract Expressionism and later inspire conceptual artists.

Other artists challenged the conventional aims and materials of art in a more Utopian spirit, embracing cultures of non-Western voices. Followers of the Theosophy Movement sought a direct, mystical experience of God and transcendent wisdom through intuition, spiritual ecstasy or revelation. Picasso gleaned psychological insight through African art. Mondrian set out to create a universal plastic language. Such influences opened up a world of new possibilities and challenges to artists. Returning to the ancient role of shaman, artists became cultural or spiritual guides whose work exceeded traditional boundaries and could best be understood by the soul, not the eye.

The Great Depression, political instability and the Second World War led to yet other appraisals of art's meaning. Jean Fautrier's *Hostage* series of paintings, completed while in hiding during the Nazi occupation of France, depicts ambiguous forms: life forms unanchored. Fine, dried pigment flecks[1] were dropped onto the wet surface of the paintings — a visual allusion to the final dust of once-mortal beings.

Jean Dubuffet, inspired by the spirit of children in a landscape of war's devastation, turned to the language of dirt and powder, the naïve, the primitive, the insane to create *art brut*, an art of power and hope. Encouraged by Dubuffet, Antoni Tàpies of Spain struggled against an oppressive religion and state to create a symbolic language of graffiti-like marks and symbols scribed onto canvases covered in layers of marble dust. Like the Theosophists, Tàpies wanted viewers of his art to be directly inspired by an emotional response, not by an intellectual assessment. Fascinated by the discoveries of modern physicists, Tàpies wrote: "Take matter, for example. I'm fascinated by the way it can be dematerialized: once you break it down and analyze it, it turns into fields of energy."[2]

The idea of matter becoming energy was by extension a concept that illuminated theories of color. Seeing a universal language in color has its roots in prehistoric and ancient artmaking. In Tibetan Tantric tradition, for example, those suffering from illness are cured by being "placed into a space of a certain shape and color, determined by the diagnosis and letting these formal properties work the cure."[3]

Yves Klein believed that by contemplating pure monochromatic colors, we could "sense the soul." Klein saw blue as "the invisible becoming visible. Blue has no dimensions."[4] His monochrome sculptures of sponges with layers of pure blue pigment held in the most delicate binding were believed by the artist and his wife to emanate vibrations or wavelengths of a vital energy.

To glimpse the visionary realm beyond our daily concerns, Rothko invites us to pass through his atmospheric color as we might enter the space of an open doorway. For Rothko, color itself could be a transcendent realm. Looking at his paintings, we hear his prophetic words, "The familiar identity of things has to be pulverized in order to destroy the finite associations with which society increasingly enshrouds every aspect of our environment."[5]

Whereas Rothko's paintings work their magic by dematerializing before our gaze, Anish Kapoor's use of color is dense, concrete and three-dimensional. In *From 1,000 Names...*, a cube drenched in red powder is juxtaposed with an orb dusted in white. Inspired by the powders he saw outside temples in India, Kapoor draws on native color symbolism, artistic color theory, and his own metaphysics. Red is readily identified with blood and the earth tones of soil. In Sanskrit, red also means *light* — the first glimmer of light at dawn before the sun rises to its apex, glows white and heats the earth. Numerous symbols of the carnal and the spiritual circle round each other in Kapoor's art. So, too, in Daisy Youngblood's clay sculpture. Here an upright seated horse is posed in a state of meditative bliss, its folded legs covered in beautiful red powder. The horse's third eye, centered mid-torso, is a symbol of pure awareness. "There is no sense of death — only the excitement of being alive in a changing form," says the artist.[6]

Pure energy and light have engaged the imagination of Mary Corse since the 1960s. Moving past her ethereal canvases containing glass microspheres — the material that makes street signs glow at night — the paintings change. The play of light gives her work an otherworldly evanescence. It's as if we could reach into and through her fields of white into another dimension, where form and space, matter and spirit, are interchangeable.

English artist Richard Long lives his art in his life. On his extensive walks through countryside and wilderness, Long arranges stone, driftwood or other found materials into cairns, circles and lines. Like the Navajo shaman, Long does not preserve these on-site works, but leaves them to their fate. He does document these experiences in photographs, stone sculptures and mud "paintings," such as the untitled example in this exhibition made of Mississippi mud. The element of time, as well as the artist's own physical involvement in the walk, in the art-making, in the hand gestures of splashing the mud, result in an art that goes beyond the visual.

Moving pastel and charcoal pictures offer silent, interwoven tales in South African artist William Kentridge's film, *Weighing and Wanting*. It is a compassionate entreaty to remember, and forgive, the storied strata of the racial, cultural and political landscape that is South Africa. Kentridge's affecting, visual narratives offer a language of hope for the world.

The ritual of leaving a mark, a rubbing, scarification, an essence to imprint memory finds its roots in worldwide traditions. Cuban-born Ana Mendieta spent years of isolation and exile as a child. As a young woman she began to create art using gunpowder, blood and mud "as a way of reclaiming my roots and joining myself with nature."[7] Mendieta's work is imbued with elements of the Santeria religion, a potent mixture of African Yoruba tribal rites and Catholicism imposed by Spanish rulers.

The interiors of David Nash's charred tree forms contain a sense of vast space. Nash chars the wood, breaking down the flesh of the tree to its mineral form — carbon — one of the products of photosynthesis, which sustains all life on earth. Just as the process of photosynthesis converts light into energy, Nash finds rebirth in the natural cycles of the tree's existence. "Worn down and regenerated; broken off and reunited; a dormant faith is revived in the new growth on an old wood."[8]

Nowhere is nature considered with more reverence and tenderness than in the works of Wolfgang Laib. With the deliberate, meditative pace of a monk, Laib gathers his raw material — such as pollen from flowers and nut trees — near his remote German village. The tiny cone of hazelnut pollen shown here required six months to gather. Then Laib slowly sifted the nearly weightless powder into its final form, releasing the energy inherent in pure color. The pollen has startling luminosity, in which both material and color are one. Light in the smallest "mote" becomes the source of an energetic presence.

The gravitational pull of deep space can be felt in the dense, obsessively drawn cosmologies of Vija Celmins. Over a period of months, Celmins layers her drawings with black charcoal of immeasurable density, leaving only tiny dots of virgin paper to form luminescent stars in her galaxies. The powdery density of charcoal is essential to Celmins' mission — to bring to our daily lives a contemplative moment to consider the infinite meanings in the night sky.

Artists have also employed powders to characterize the gritty reality of a contemporary urban world. Katharina Fritsch's iconic urban *Rattenkönig (Rat-King)*, a ring of 16 life-sized, cast polyester rats, are veiled in a sooty film of black powder. Each rat, as it would in nature, curls its tail around its neighbor's to form a knot — a telegraphic, protective, ironic social symbol.

Irony sifts it way on to an open copy of Djuna Barnes' novel, *Nightwood*, in the installation piece of the same title by Rebecca Horn. The novelist's tale of a lesbian, which suffered repeated attempts at censure before finally being published, is here slowly dusted in white face powder. Horn exposes with incisive wit the oppressiveness of society. English artist Cornelia Parker exposes the impotence of cliché when she starches a folded pile of white cotton sheets with chalk from her native White Cliffs of Dover. The soft sheets, interlaced with Dover chalk, become stiff, like the cliffs themselves. Images meant to reassure, such as bed sheets, and the symbolic presence of the Cliffs of Dover, also kindle a fear of sleep, of nightmares, of heights and loss.

Some powdered materials can be both benign and lethal, like medicines that in small doses can cure and in larger quantities can kill. In Man Ray's early photographs, such as *Dust Breeding* (1920), the artist captures a chaotic web of presumably benign microscopic dust. Sigmar Polke creates a "chemical theatre" in which unstable materials are suspended in different mediums. Polke's seemingly ambiguous images force us to "see afresh" the multitude of meanings in invisible and corrosive substances of a nuclear age in which fallout and its aftermath are a constant threat. His complex imagemaking is both misleading and revealing.

Anselm Kiefer's free intermingling of mythic and real narratives reflects the artist's belief that there are no truths, only interpretations. His use of fragile materials and alchemy is symbolic of a state of spiritual anxiety in which matter changing form can transform into imminent chaos. Kiefer's hope is that on reflection, without his direct intervention, mankind will evolve to a more advanced spiritual state.

Shadow by Andy Warhol, both seductive and diaphanous, abstract and common, is a shape in a haze of luminous "diamond dust" (in actuality, crushed commercial glass). No critic of Warhol's work could agree on an interpretation of the *Shadow* series, nor were they helped by Warhol's own evasive, sometimes contradictory answers to questions about his work.[9]

Criss-crossed in fluid patterns, Juan Uslé's stream-of-consciousness paintings suggest a new language, one not burdened with the weight of established meanings. Powders on his layered canvases express dispersal, contradiction and flux. Suzanne McClelland's raw canvases are buried and then recovered. Each canvas contains a fine imprint of mold and bacterial growth that leaves a drawing in the fiber, setting the stage for an intuitive response by the artist. Layers of patterns and messages are then developed with a wide range of pigments and powdered materials in paintings with a welter of narratives. Brazilian artist Rivane Neuenschwander transforms an everyday domestic vocabulary of a woman's world — flour, garlic, seeds, nylons, incense — into double-edged metaphors that are existential, aesthetic and political.

Jackie Winsor's sculptures conceal, then reveal, their secrets, though only after scrutiny on the viewer's part. The black exterior of *Burned and Red Inside-Out Piece* was originally its interior, which Winsor burned to charcoal black. The cube was then "forced apart at its seams and put back together inside out. I was interested in emotional and physical vulnerability as part of strength. Part of the strength of this piece is its anchored presence and the echo of its history of transformed vulnerability."[10]

Photographing his sand tracks, balanced rocks, ice spirals, clouds of dust or sprays of water thrown into the air, English artist Andy Goldsworthy produces ephemeral artworks: snowballs that melt, leaving behind dirt washes; icicles made and frozen around trees, and "rain shadows" in which the artist creates a dry silhouette where his own body keeps rain from hitting the ground. Goldsworthy uses forms in nature to create sculpture, yet his reliance on improvisation and chance never imposes itself on nature.

The language of powders can be sublime for the sake of pure aesthetic. In Jennifer Bartlett's drawings for the Homan-ji temple in Choshi, near Tokyo, the artist synthesizes the Buddhist tradition with the cultural life of contemporary Japan. Her body of work incorporates an ancient traditional use of pure mineral pigments that are timeless. Elizabeth Murray's application of pure pastel on shaped papers is a departure from the historic use of the medium, resulting in a very personal vocabulary of forms that demand scrutiny. Roni Horn's drawings of sculptural forms suggest architecture, material density and visceral physicality. The obsessive build-up of graphite on the undulating drawings of Nancy Rubins implies action, violence, and relentless energy, signifying movement and containment, permanence and fragility.

It is fitting that the termination of the entire era of the dinosaurs 65 million years ago is condensed to a fine strata of powder less than an inch deep around the earth, indicating the impact of that fateful meteor. The grottoes of Lascaux (circa 15,000 BC), coated by early man in brilliant pigments to record their world, today are sealed off from the public to protect them from polluting dust. These works also draw attention to the fragility of our world. Dust, the source of life as well as its denouement, is both healing and toxic. Using a sparse but potent vocabulary of reductive materials we may contemplate a body of work in which intuition, emotion and alchemy are as important as the source of their chosen materials.

In an attempt to bring together seemingly opposing messages, we recall the words of Wolfgang Laib, "If you believe only in the individual, in what you are, then life is a tragedy that ends in death. But if you feel part of a whole, that what you are doing is not just you, the individual, but something bigger, then all these problems are not there any more. Everything is totally different."[11]

1   See Ponge, Francis, *Notes sur les Otages. Peinture de Fautrier* (Pierre Seghers, 1946). Our thanks to Susan Davidson, Associate Curator, and Carol Marcuso Ungaro, Chief Conservator, the Menil Collection, Houston, for their examination of the painting, *Oradour-sur-Glane* (1945) by Jean Fautrier, and confirmation of dry flecked pigment on the painted surface.

2   Tapiès, Antoni, as found in Peppiatt, Michael, "Antoni Tapiès: Fields of Energy," *Art International* (Summer 1988), p. 37.

3   McEvilley, Thomas, "Medicine Man: Proposing a Context for Wolfgang Laib's Work," *Parkett*, No. 39, 1994, pp. 104–109 English text; pp. 110–117 German text.

4   Klein, Yves, as found in McEvilley, Thomas, "Yves Klein and Rosicrucianism," *Yves Klein: A Retrospective* (The Rice Museum and The Arts Publisher, 1981).

5   Rothko, Mark, *Possibilities* (1947), as found in Chipp, Herschel B. (ed.), *Theories of Modern Art: A Source Book by Artists and Critics* (University of California Press, 1968).

6   In a conversation with the authors, December 6, 1998.

7   Mendieta, Ana, as found in Aliaga, Juan Vincente, "Ana Mendieta," *Frieze* Nov.–Dec. 1996), pp. 85–86.

8   Nash, David, as found in *David Nash, Forms into Time* (Academy Group Ltd., 1996), p. 25.

9   Smith, Patrick, *Andy Warhol's Art and Films*, (UMI Research Press, 1981), pg. 200.

10 Correspondence with the authors, December 6, 1998.

11 Laib, Wolfgang, as found in Farrow, Clare, "Wolfgang Laib: More than Myself," *Parkett*, No. 39, 1994, p. 80.

JENNIFER BARTLETT

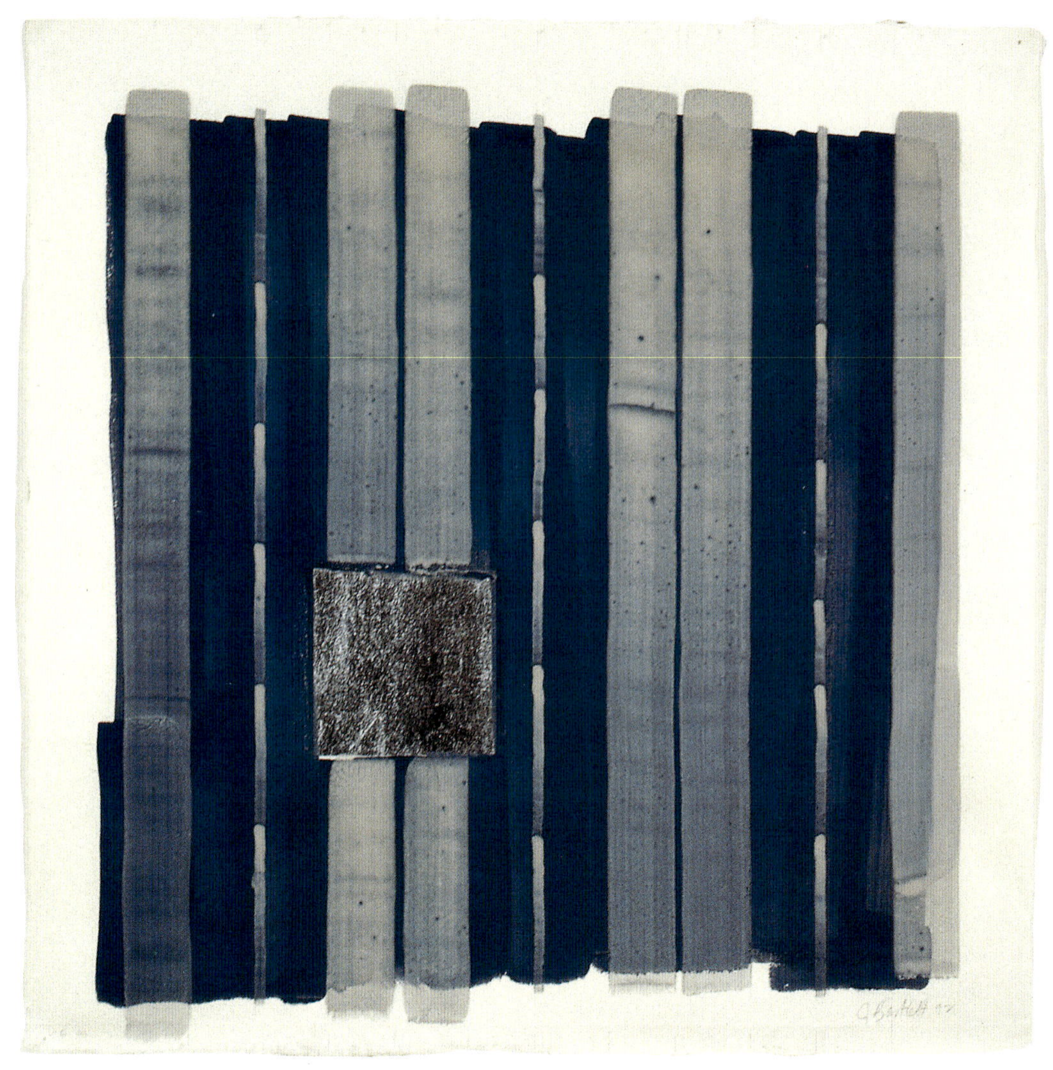

Homan-J; Series II, V-6   1992
Japanese mineral color on handmade Kozo paper
25⅛" x 25⅛"
Collection Peggy and Dick Danziger, New York

Vija Celmins

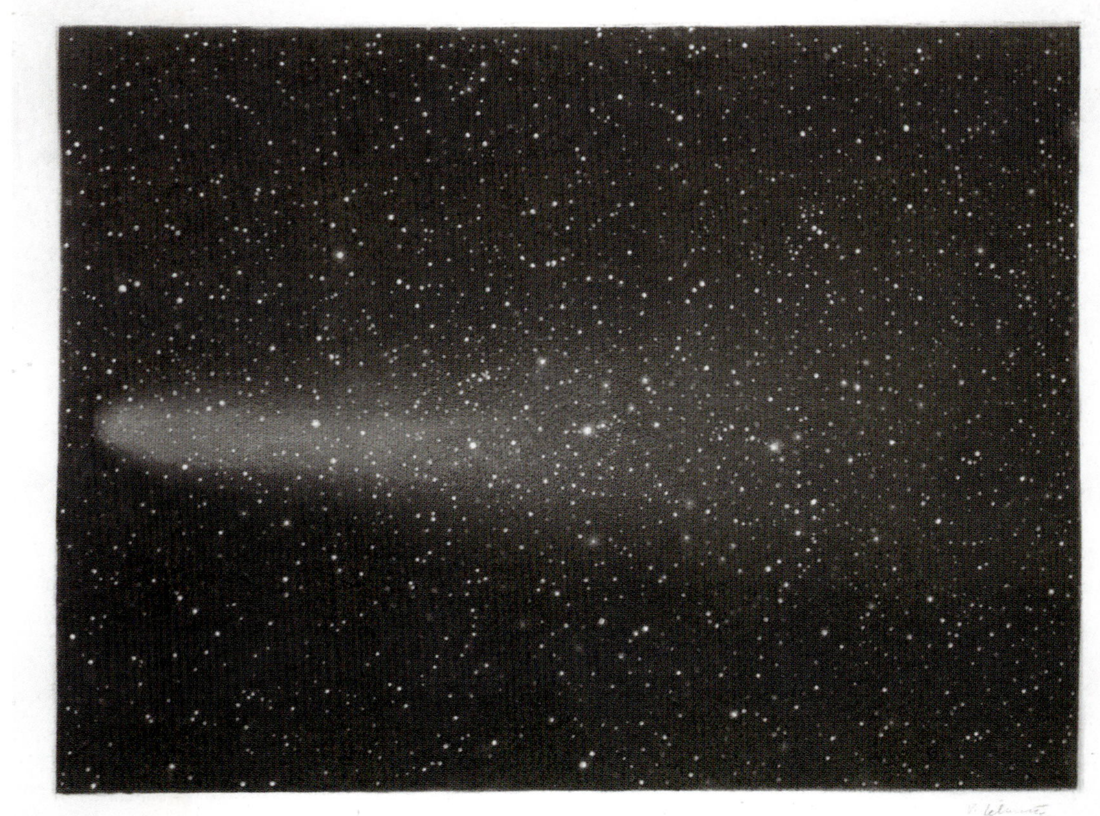

Untitled #10 1994-95
charcoal on paper
17⅛" x 22⅛"
Collection of David and Renee McKee, New York

"I think there's something profound about working in material that is stronger than words, and is about some other place which is a little more mysterious." Vija Celmins, as quoted in Berger, John. *Penelope as Painter*, TATE (Summer 1997), p. 85.

born 1903 Nyack, New York died 1972 New York

JOSEPH CORNELL

(from his diary, on the gathering of materials) April 15, 1946 "One of best days at home (feeling right without having to get away). Carried over with little sleep from Sunday worked late on one box in cellar… Had satisfactory feeling about cleaning up debris on cellar floor — 'sweepings' represent all the rich cross-currents, ramifications that go into the boxes but which are not apparent (I feel at least) in the final result." Cornell Papers. AAA, 1059:8–9. 107 April 15. 1946.

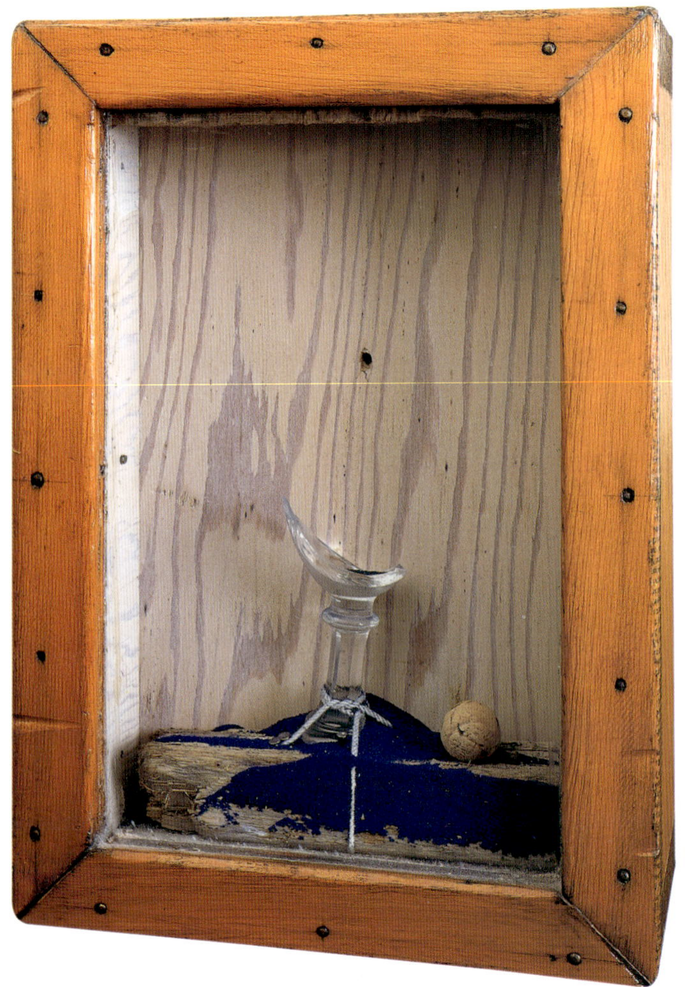

Untitled (Blue Sand Fountain) circa 1960
mixed media box construction
11½" x 8" x 4"
Private collection
Courtesy Allan Stone Gallery, New York

born 1945 Berkeley, California

MARY CORSE

"Inspired by the vision of a painting being a field of light dependent on the viewer's perception, I searched for a material that would allow me to not only put the optics of light in the painting but also in the moment of observation. The micro-glass spheres create a prism in relation to the light, the eye and the surface, so as a person moves, the painting changes; the viewer creates the painting." December 5, 1998.

White Light Painting (from the Bevel Series) 1994
micro-glass spheres in paint on canvas
48" x 48"
Courtesy Ace Gallery, New York

born 1901 LeHavre, France died 1985 Paris, France

JEAN DUBUFFET

"Mud, waste and dirt, man's companions throughout his life, should they not be his most treasured possession? And is it not a service to remind him of their beauty? See how young children look in streams through rubbish to find a thousand wonders." *Jean Dubuffet, 'L'Auteur répond à quelques objections'. Mirobolus. Macadam et Cie.. Paris. 1946.*

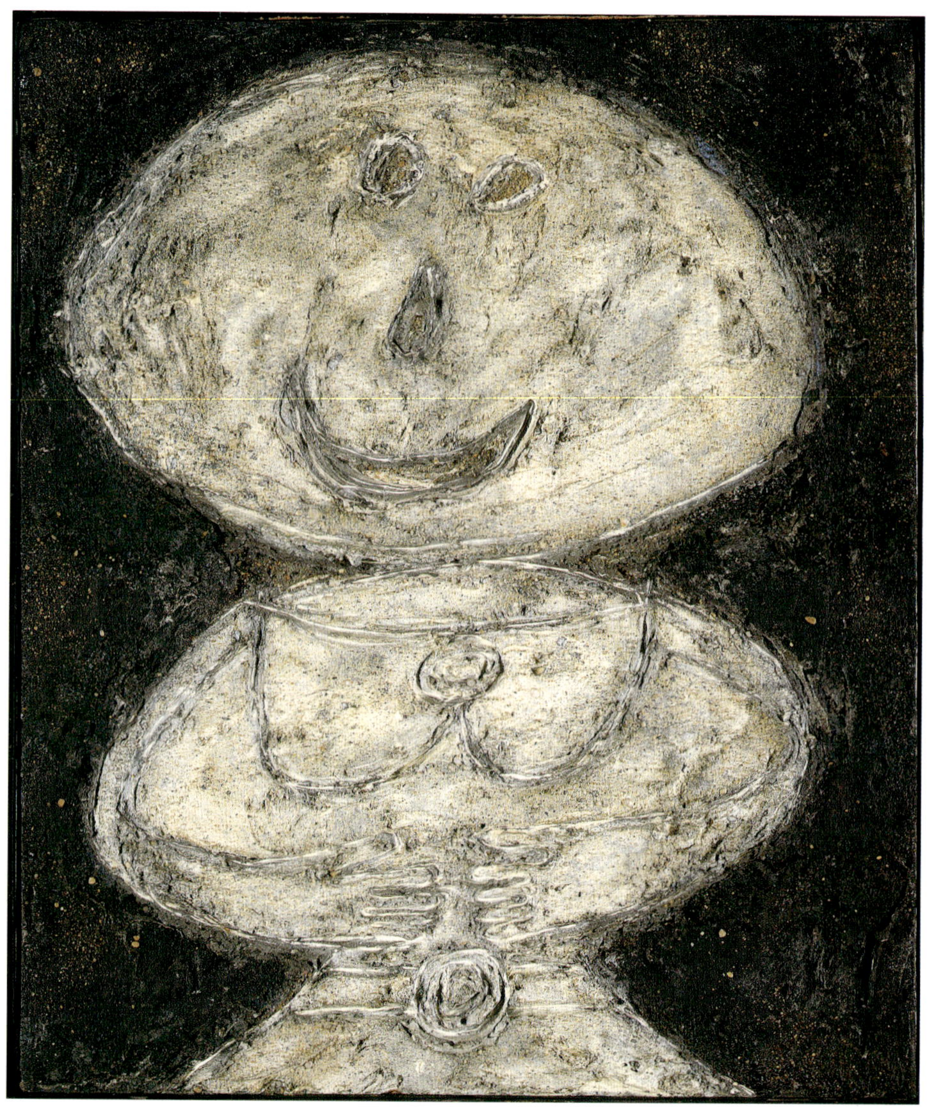

Bouche en croissant ou Rieuse à bouche en croissant de lune
(Crescent Mouth, or Laughing Woman with a Crescent-Moon Mouth) 1946
oil, pebbles and sand on canvas
25⅝" x 21¼"
National Gallery of Art, Washington
The Stephen Hahn Family Collection (Partial and Promised Gift)
Photograph ©1998 Board of Trustees, National Gallery of Art, Washington
Photo: Bob Grove

born 1956 Essen, Germany

KATHARINA FRITSCH

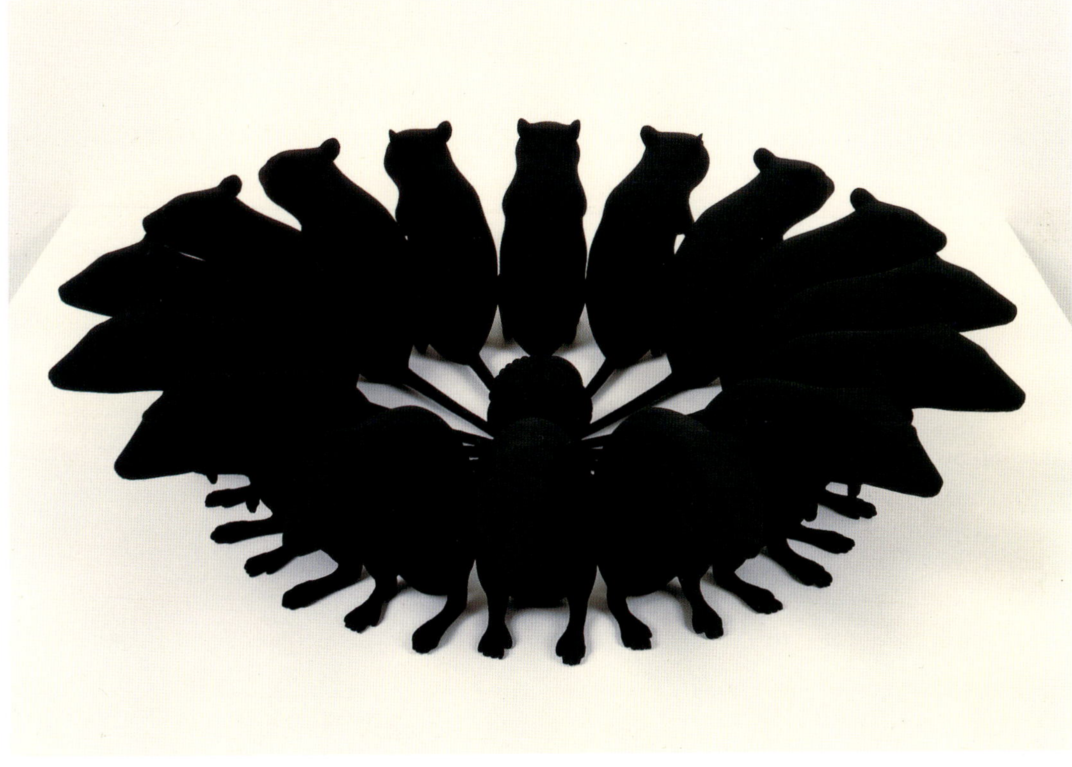

Rattenkönig (Rat-King) 1998
polyester and paint; edition of eight
5⅞" x 23⅝" diameter
Courtesy Matthew Marks Gallery, New York
Photo: Nic Tenwiggenhorn
©1999 Artists Rights Society (ARS), New York/VG Bild-Kunst, Bonn

"Why does everything have to come back to concepts? Being disturbed visually, experiencing ambivalence — why does that have to go straight into the language cage? It's just an escape into didacticism. A really important element in my work is that you come in, experience an image, allow yourself to be drawn into it, perceive it directly." Winzen, Matthias. *In conversation with Katherine Fritsch*, San Francisco Museum of Modern Art. (October 1996–March 1997).

born 1956 Cheshire, England

ANDY GOLDSWORTHY

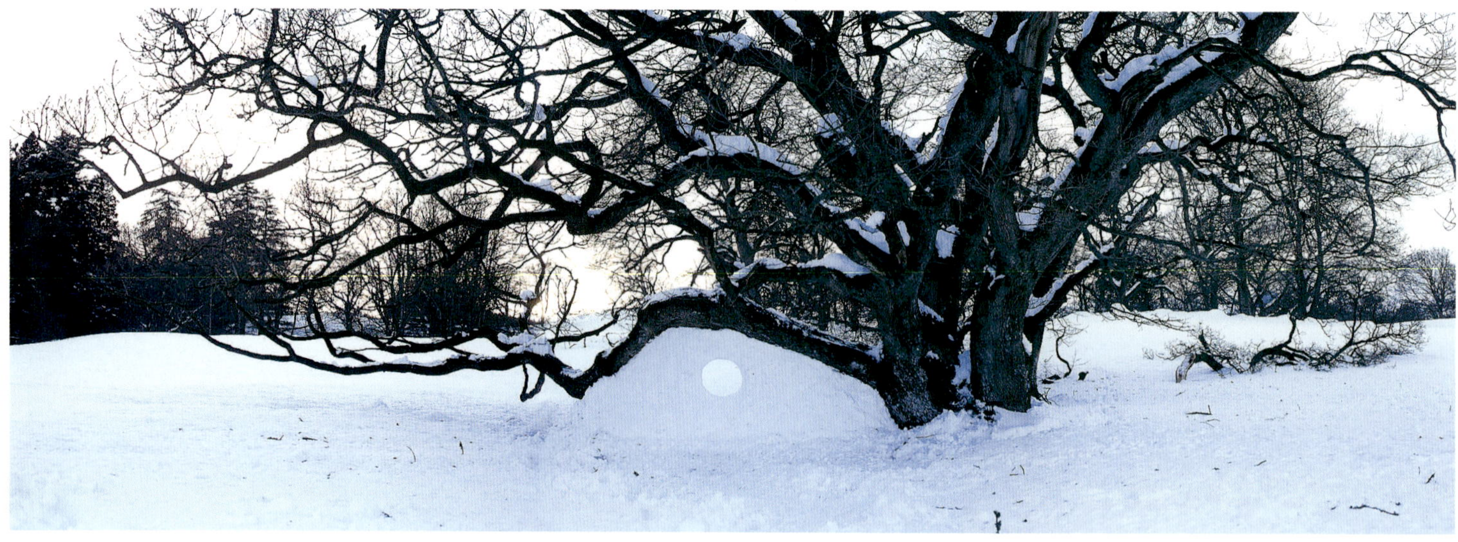

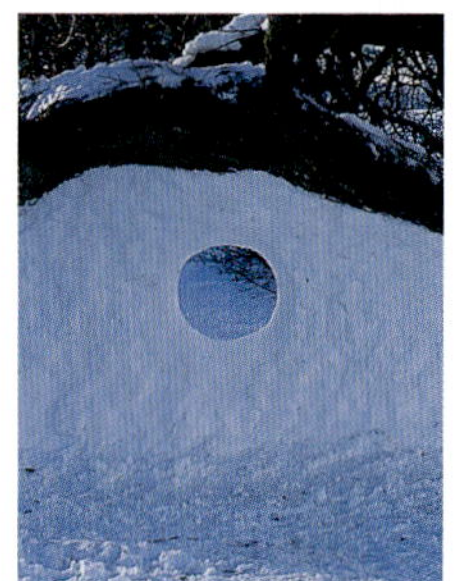 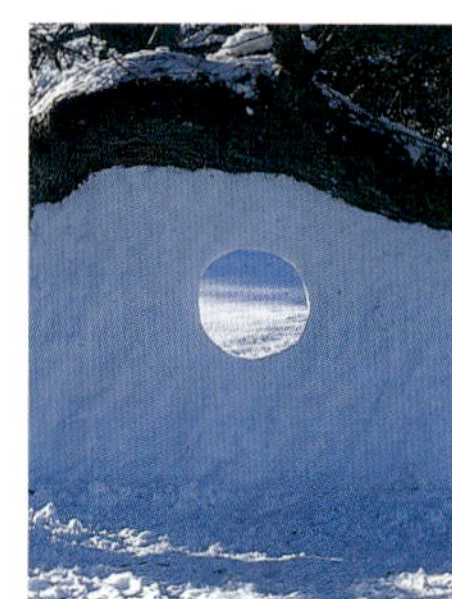 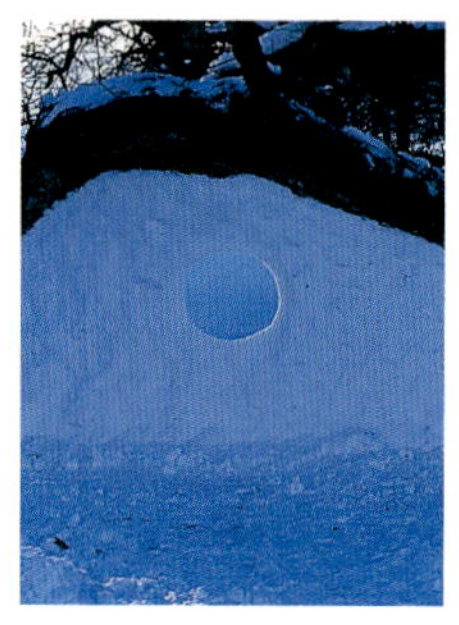 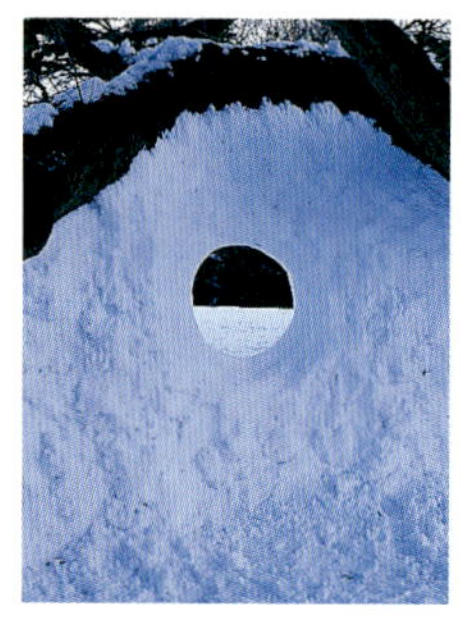 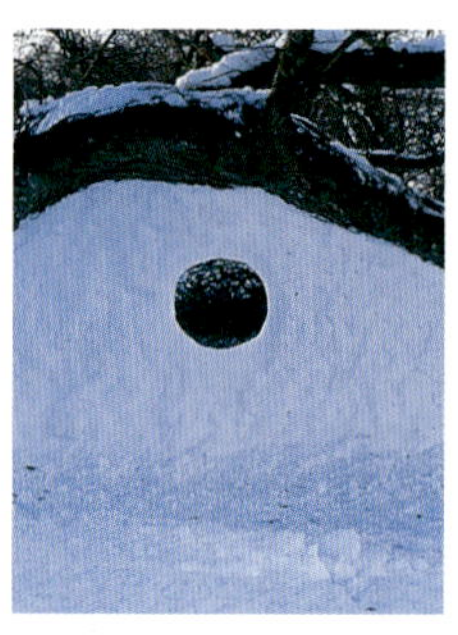 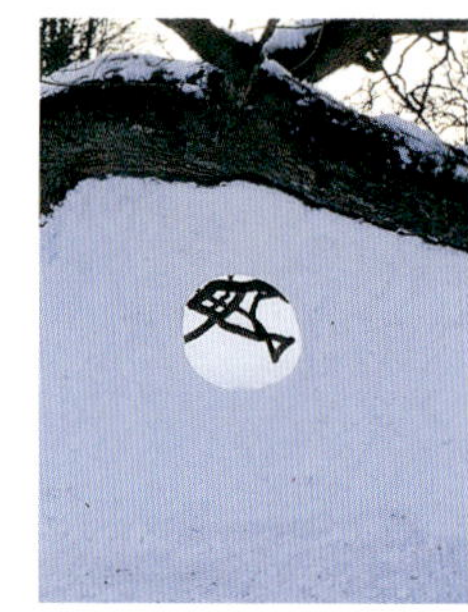

Filled in under the branch arch with snow made
a hole that changed the light (2/8/96)
nine photographs
31½" x 63¾" large photo
Collection Zoe and Joel Dictrow, New York,
Courtesy Galerie Lelong, New York
Photo: Courtesy Michael Hue-Williams
Fine Art, Ltd., London

"I have worked with red earth in many places. It flows around the earth as a vein. It is red because of its iron content which is also why our blood is red. The red in blood is related to breath, and breath is what we share with vegetation." Friedman, Terry, *WOOD Andy Goldsworthy*, Harry N. Abrams, Inc. Publishers, NY, Copyright © 1996 Andy Goldsworthy, (photography and text) and Cameron Books, p. 15.

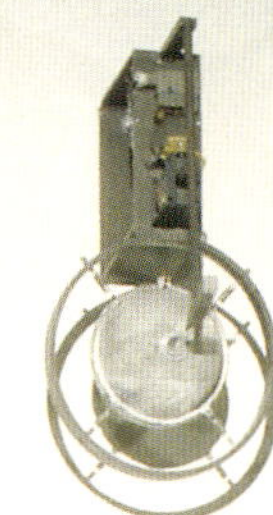

REBECCA HORN

Nightwood – Djuna Barnes 1990
motor, sieve, hammer, face powder, book, steel
139½" x 12" x 12"
Courtesy Marian Goodman Gallery, New York
Photo: Guy L'Heureux

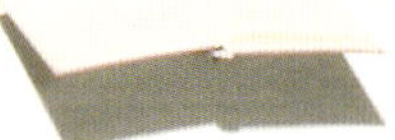

"The sculptures in an installation encapsulate stories and experience, they are living experience crystallized into a kind of chemical formula." A conversation with Rebecca Horn, from *Rebecca Horn, The Glance of Infinity*, ed. Carl Haenlein, Scalo Verlag, 1997.

RONI HORN

"The choice to use pigment is the choice to use matter." December 4, 1998.

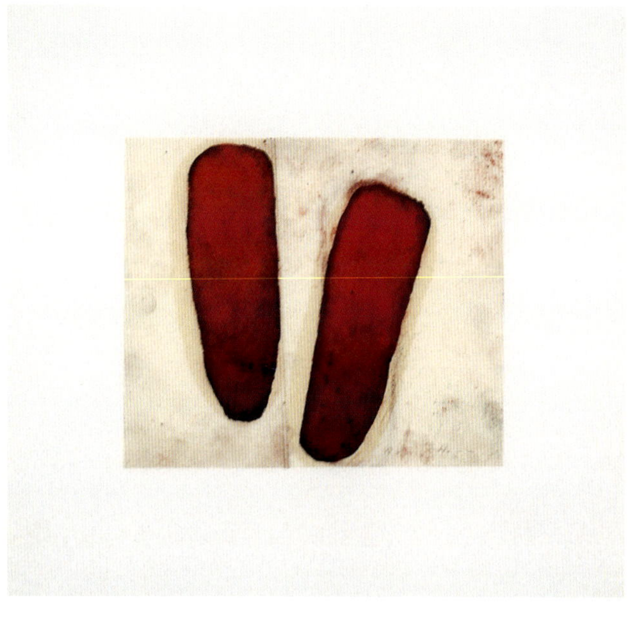

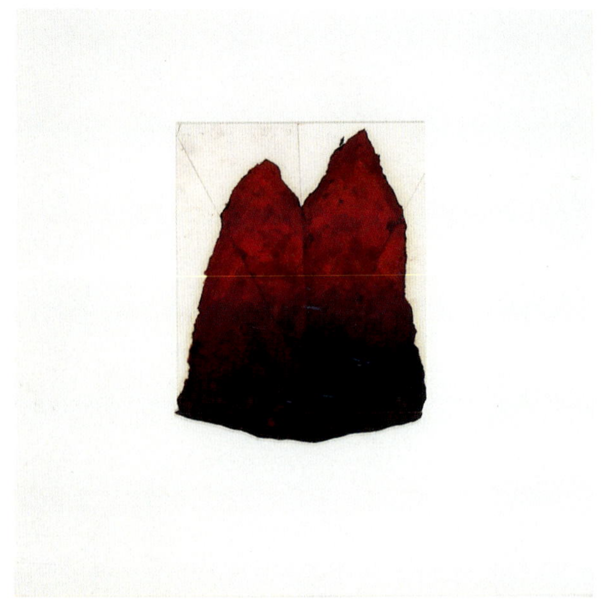

Untitled 1985
powdered pigment, varnish on paper
mounted on board
4⅝" x 6"
Collection Amy and Richard Lipton

Untitled 1985
powdered pigment, varnish on paper
mounted on board
7¼" x 6¼"
Collection Amy and Richard Lipton

born 1954 Bombay, India

ANISH KAPOOR

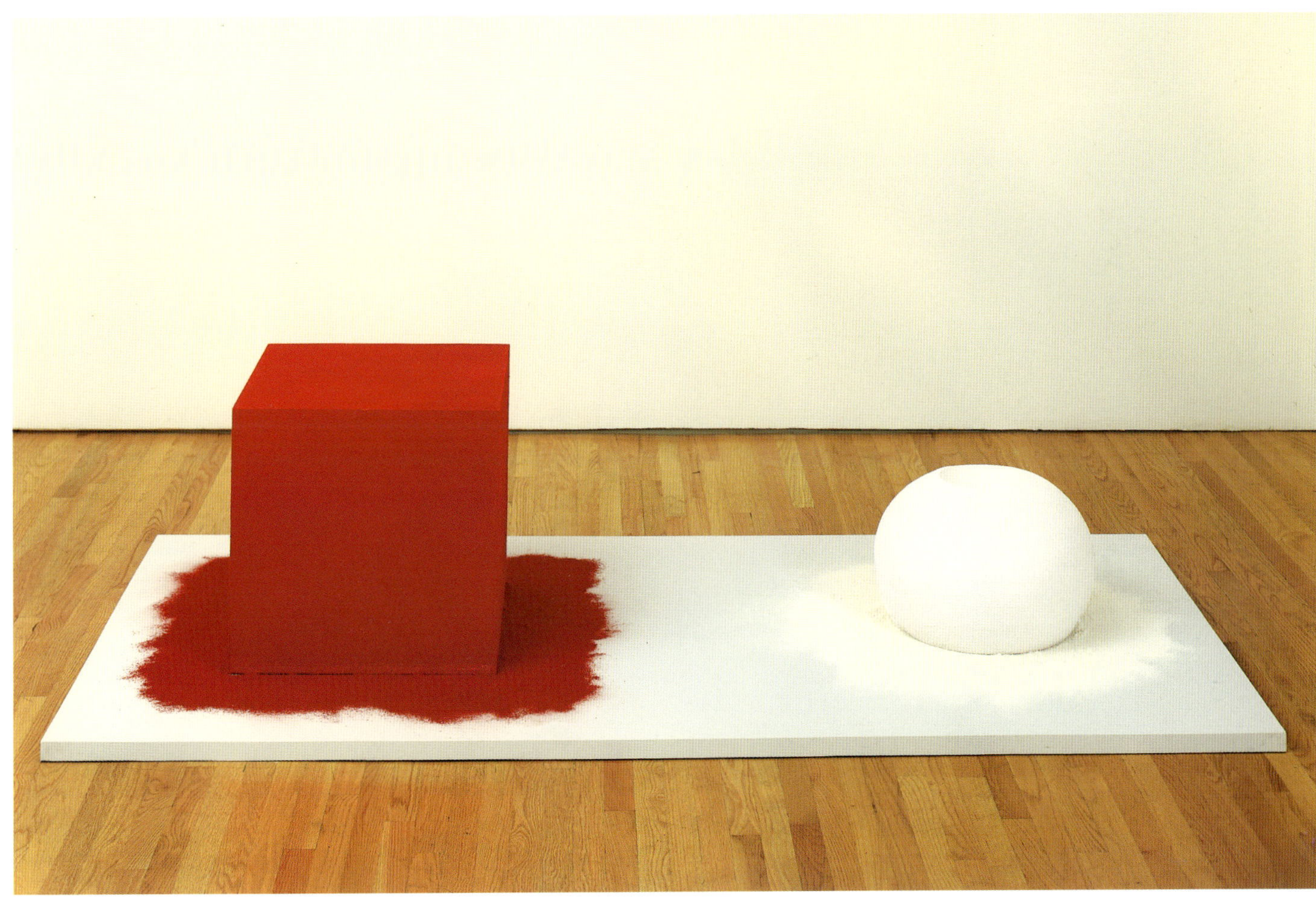

From 1000 Names… 1979-1980
wood, plaster, pigment
24" x 58" x 24"
Courtesy Barbara Gladstone Gallery, New York
Photo: David Regen

…"what I'm looking for is a condition of yellowness or a condition of redness that is so clear that it is like
wetness or heaviness. It has to do with intensity, saturation and a certain kind of completeness. Absoluteness."
Andrew, Lambirth, "Embrace the Void," *The Independent: Saturday Magazine* (1998), p.36.

born 1955 Johannesburg, South Africa

WILLIAM KENTRIDGE

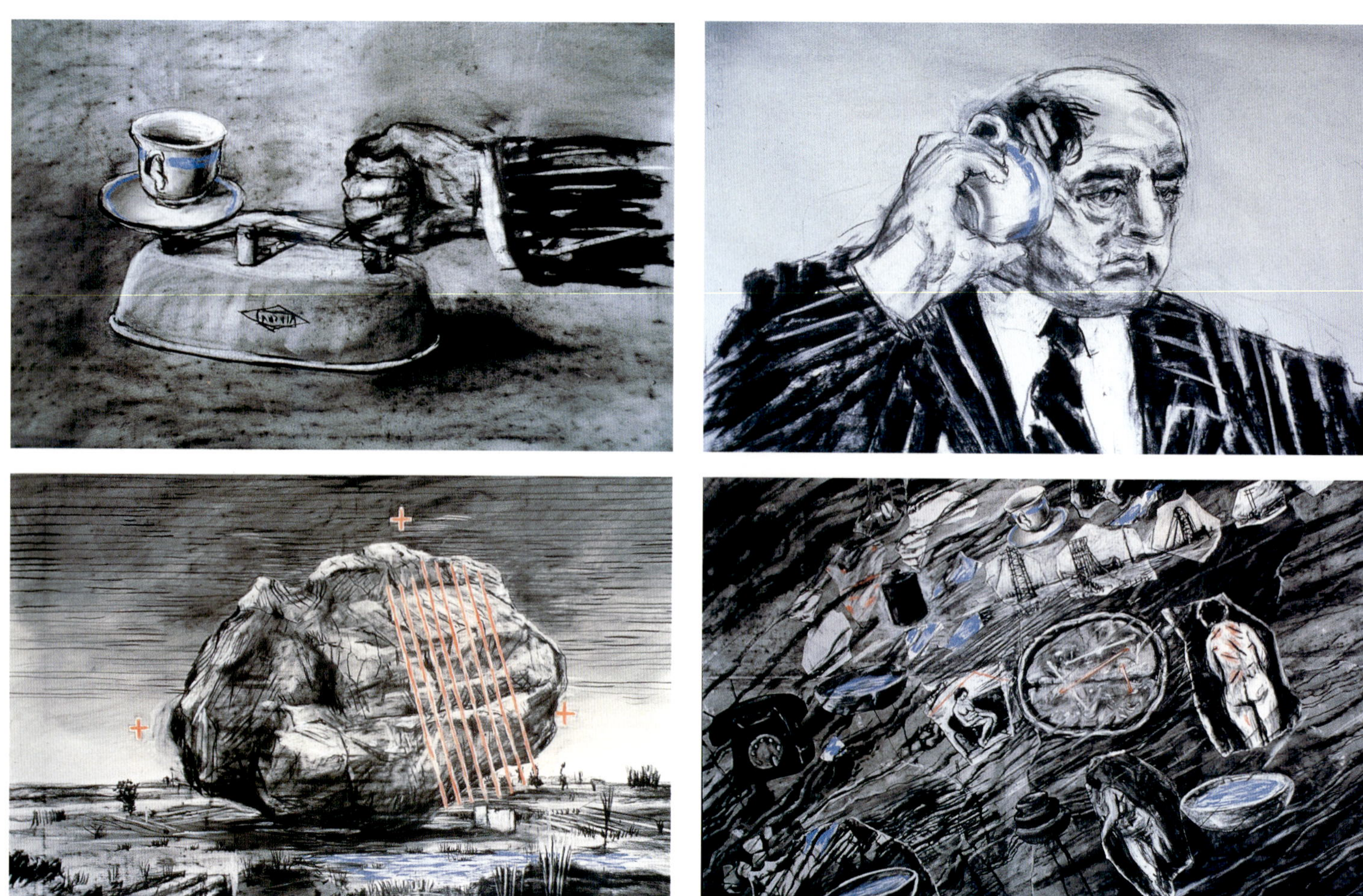

Weighing and Wanting
image 9'10½" x 6'6¾"
room size 19'8" x 13'1½"
videotape
Courtesy Marian Goodman Gallery, New York

"One of the features of charcoal is that it is both dark and adheres to the paper lightly — so something that can both be emphatic and easily erasable or changeable at the same time. One can construct an image in the way that one thinks — changing it, testing hypotheses, restructuring with one brush of a cloth, letting the flexible material lead one to clarity of thought." December 8. 1998.

YVES KLEIN

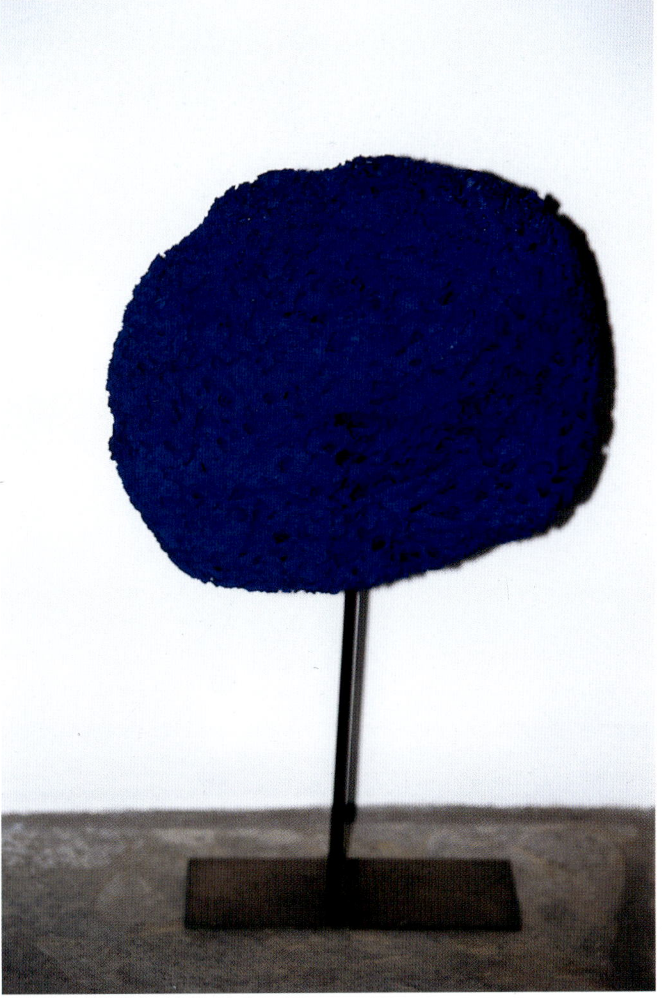

Sponge (Blue Sculpture) 1960
blue painted sponge and metal; brass pedestal
6" x 8" x 6¾"
Nancy and Bob Magoon Collection
Photo: Hal Williams Photography

"I disliked colors ground in oil. They seemed dead to me; what pleased me above all were pure pigments, in powder....Before one of my color surfaces the ideal onlooker would become, only as regards his sensitivity of course, 'extradimensional' to the point of being 'all in all' saturated with the sensitivity of the universe." As quoted in *Zero* No. 3 (July 1961), Otto Piene and Heinz Mack (eds.), *Zero* (Cambridge, Mass.: MIT Press, 1973), pp. 91–95.

Koo Jeong-a

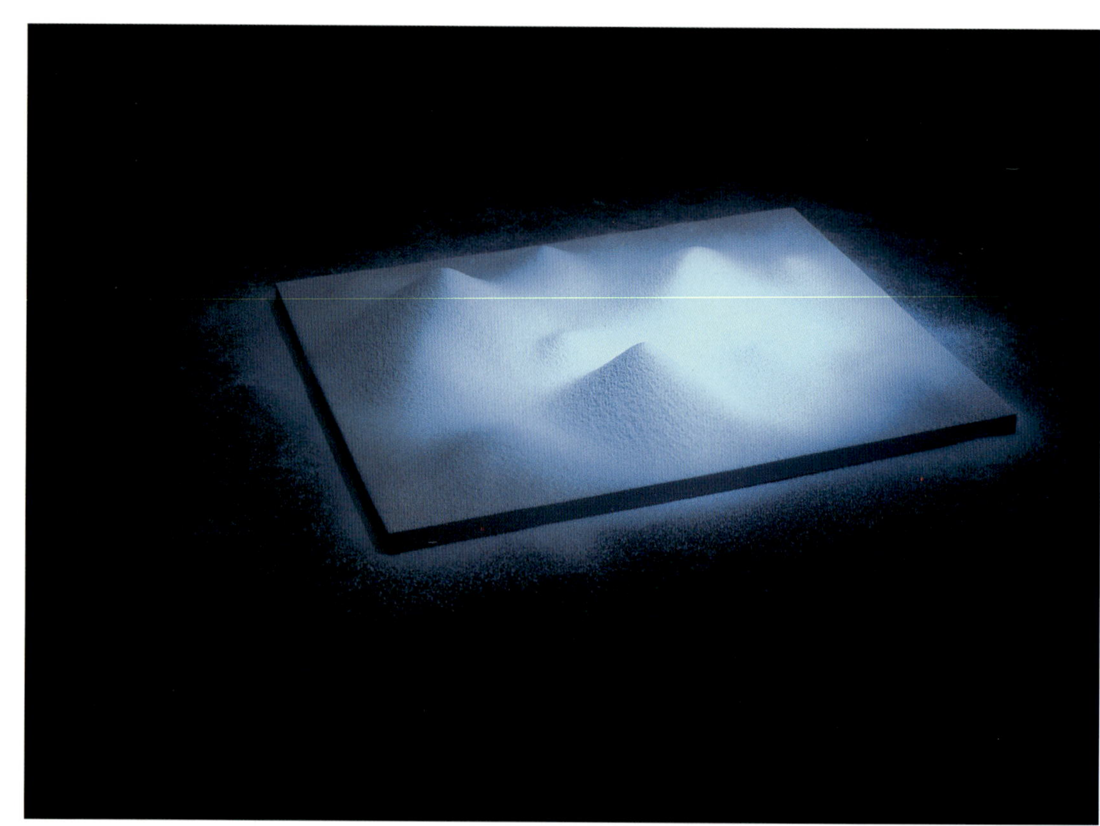

Oslo 1997
aspirin
4" x 36" x 30"
Courtesy the artist and Barbara Gladstone Gallery, New York
Photo: David Regen

"In a cupboard, on shelves, lines and lots of mothballs. Form becomes simplified syntax of a foreign language, pre-verbal, a time space continuum, a way of writing about and with things." Koo Jeong-a on *Armoire de pull-over*, 21.22.23 Mai, Paris, 1996.

"This partial inventory is insufficient to illustrate the extent to which Koo Jeong-a's work falls within the methodological search for another vocabulary, to express the temporal, the ephemeral, the disappearing, the invisible — it silently builds the foundations of an imaginary geography..." Stephene Moisdon Trembly, independent curator and art critic, Paris "On Koo Jeong-a", *Make*, Issue 80, June–August 1998.

born 1950 Metzingen, Germany

WOLFGANG LAIB

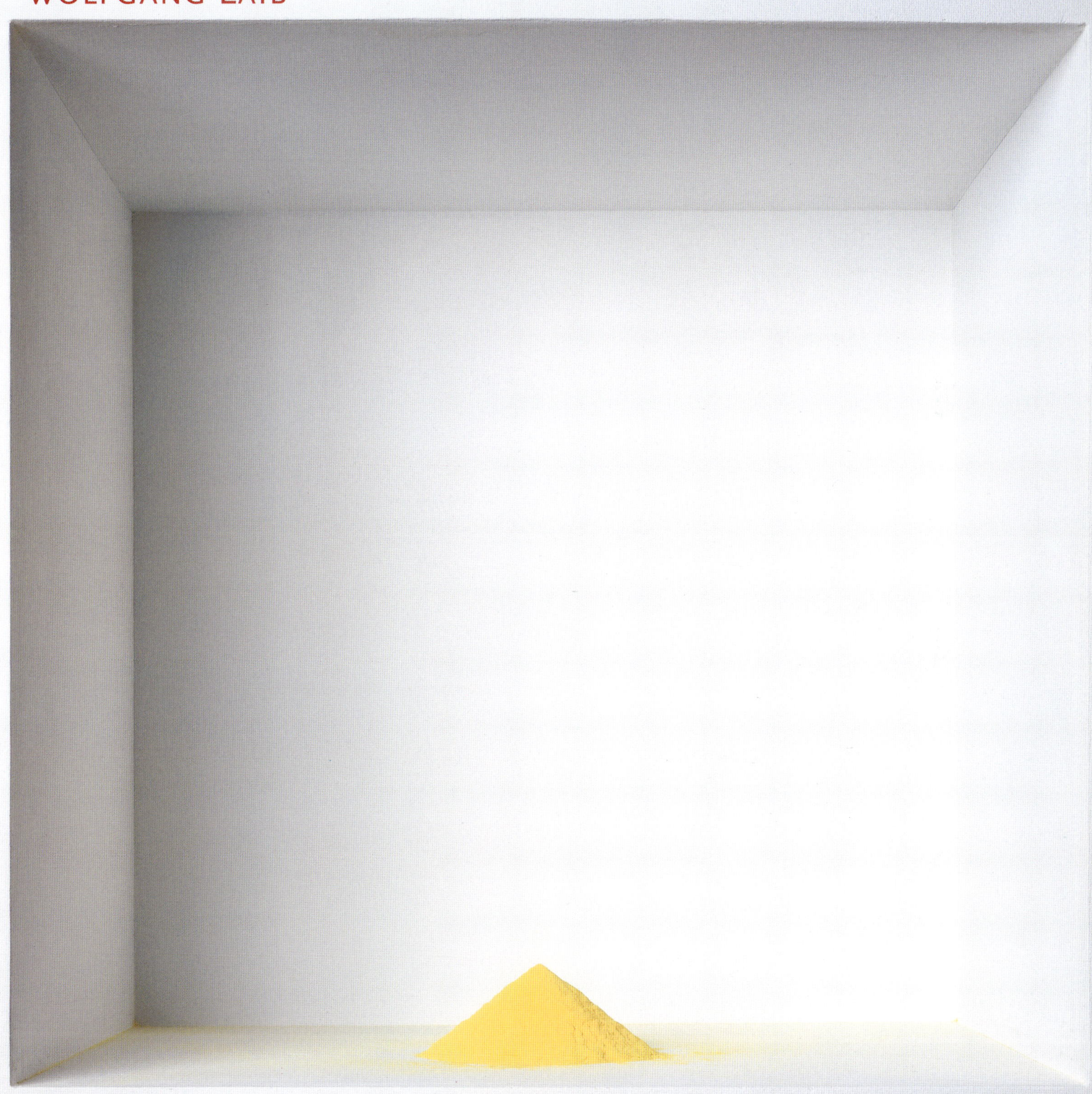

"The pollen is all the things you have said but maybe it is also many more things, things that maybe I don't know and you don't know…the pollen is what pollen is, and I am somehow participating in that, and trying to get close to these things. I could not create something like this. Which is why I…collect and sift the pollen, because I know that there is much more than myself." Farrow, Claire, *Wolfgang Laib: More than Myself, Parkett*, No. 39, 1994, pp. 77-81 English text; pp. 82-87 German text.

Untitled 1998
hazelnut pollen
2¾" high
Courtesy Sperone Westwater Gallery,
New York

born 1947 Sri Lanka

JULIAN LETHBRIDGE

"I have applied graphite to the surface of the painting and in a sense it becomes a graphite-plated painting. This thin, even layer of graphite removes all variations except changes in the surface of the painting so that the image, in this painting, is carried only on its surface." December 7, 1998.

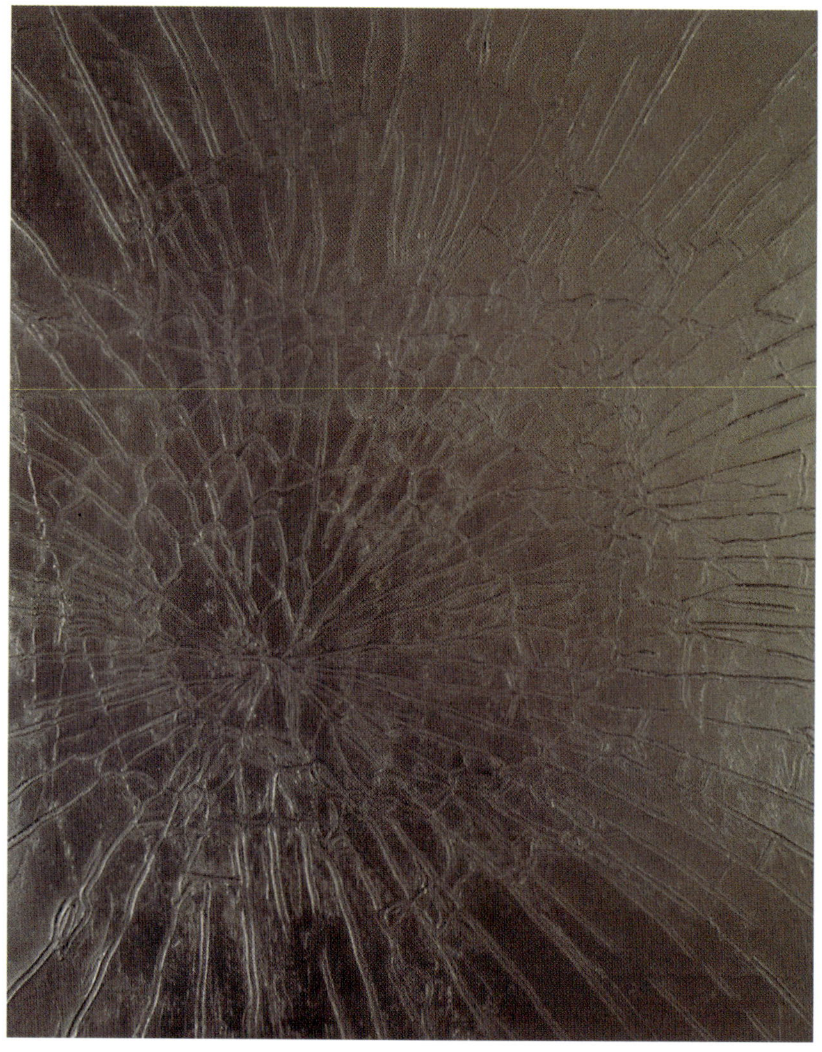

Untitled 1994-95
oil, graphite on linen
20⅛" x 16"
Courtesy the artist and Paula Cooper Gallery, New York

Maya Lin

born 1959 Athens, Ohio

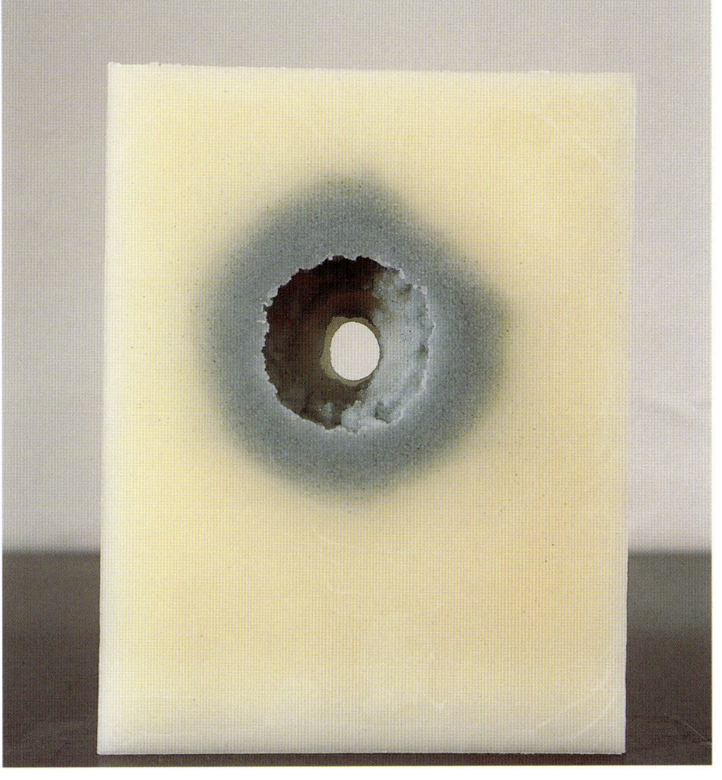

Untitled (Crater Series) 1998
beeswax and glass beads
9" x 7" x 1½"
Courtesy the artist and Gagosian Gallery, New York

"…looking at our environment through aerial photographs, satellite images, microscopic and stop camera motion has given us, in this century, a new way of seeing our world. And it is this somewhat technologically based method of analyzing or looking at the landscape that has been a significant influence on my work both in the studio sculptures as well as larger outdoor artworks."

Maya Lin, as found in Brenson, Michael, "Maya Lin's Time," *Maya Lin: Topologies,* Southeastern Center for Contemporary Art, org. by Jeff Fleming (1998), p. 38.

RICHARD LONG

Untitled 1991
Mississippi mud on paper
78" x 43⅛"
Chase Manhattan Collection
Photo: Courtesy Sperone Westwater Gallery, New York

born 1959 Jacksonville, Florida

SUZANNE McCLELLAND

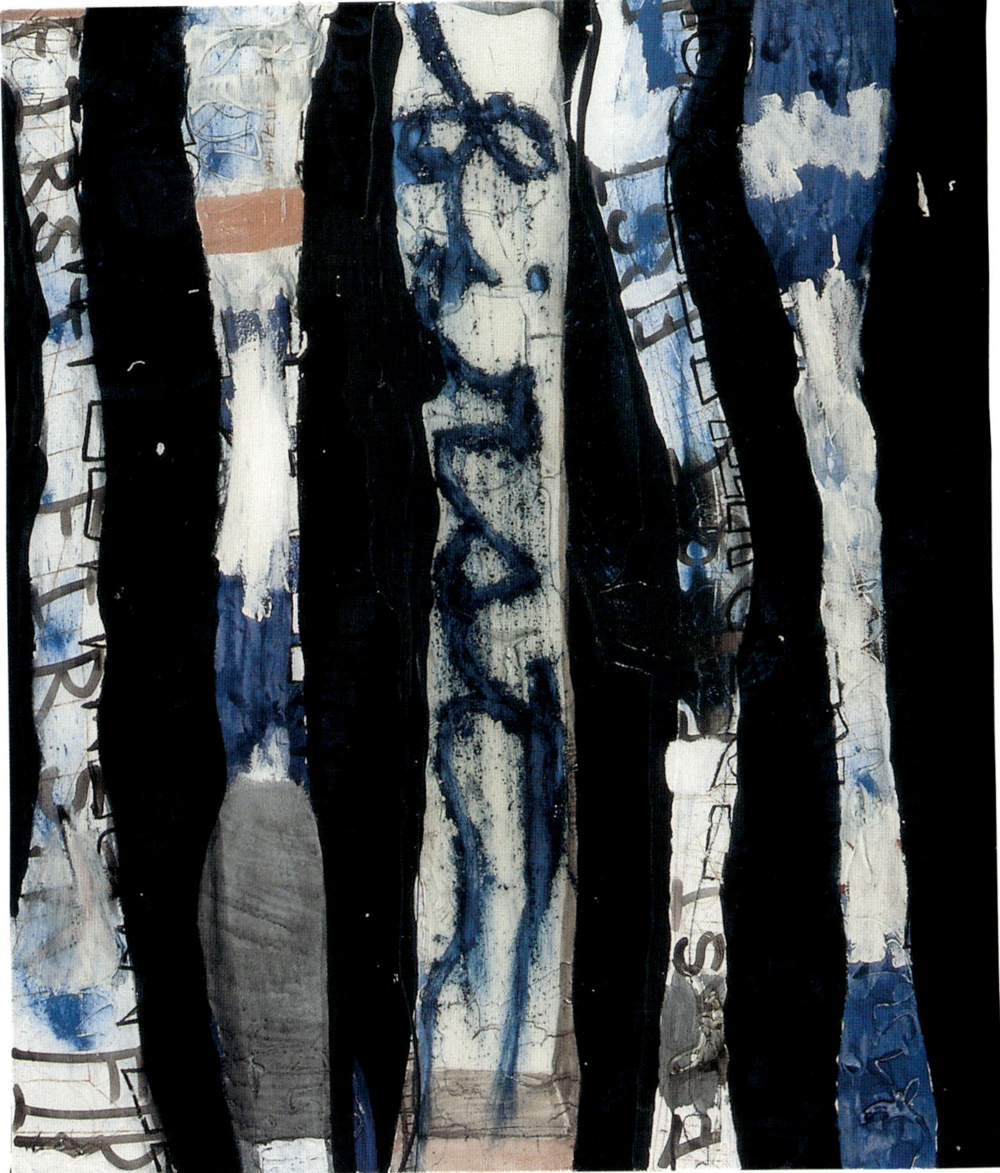

First 1998
absorbent ground, enamel, polymer emulsion, acrylic,
charcoal, dry pigment and conte on canvas
48" x 40"
Courtesy Weaver Collection, Michigan

"Years ago I tried to find a way to write very slowly in clay. Then I needed to separate the color from the carrier (fluid – extender – binder). The dry pigment started out as dirt (mud = water plus dirt) then metal, aluminum and copper which became shiny with water and changed color. Dry pigments are without form until gravity or wind make it into an image." December 3, 1998.

ANA MENDIETA

"The exploration of the relation between myself and nature that I have created in my artistic production is a clear result of the fact that I was plucked out of my adolescence. To inscribe my silhouette into nature maintains (or establishes) the transition between my country of origin and my new home. It is a way of reclaiming my roots and joining myself with nature." Ana Mendieta, as quoted in Aliaga, Juan Vincente, "Ana Mendieta," *Frieze* (Nov.- Dec. 1996), pp. 85-86.

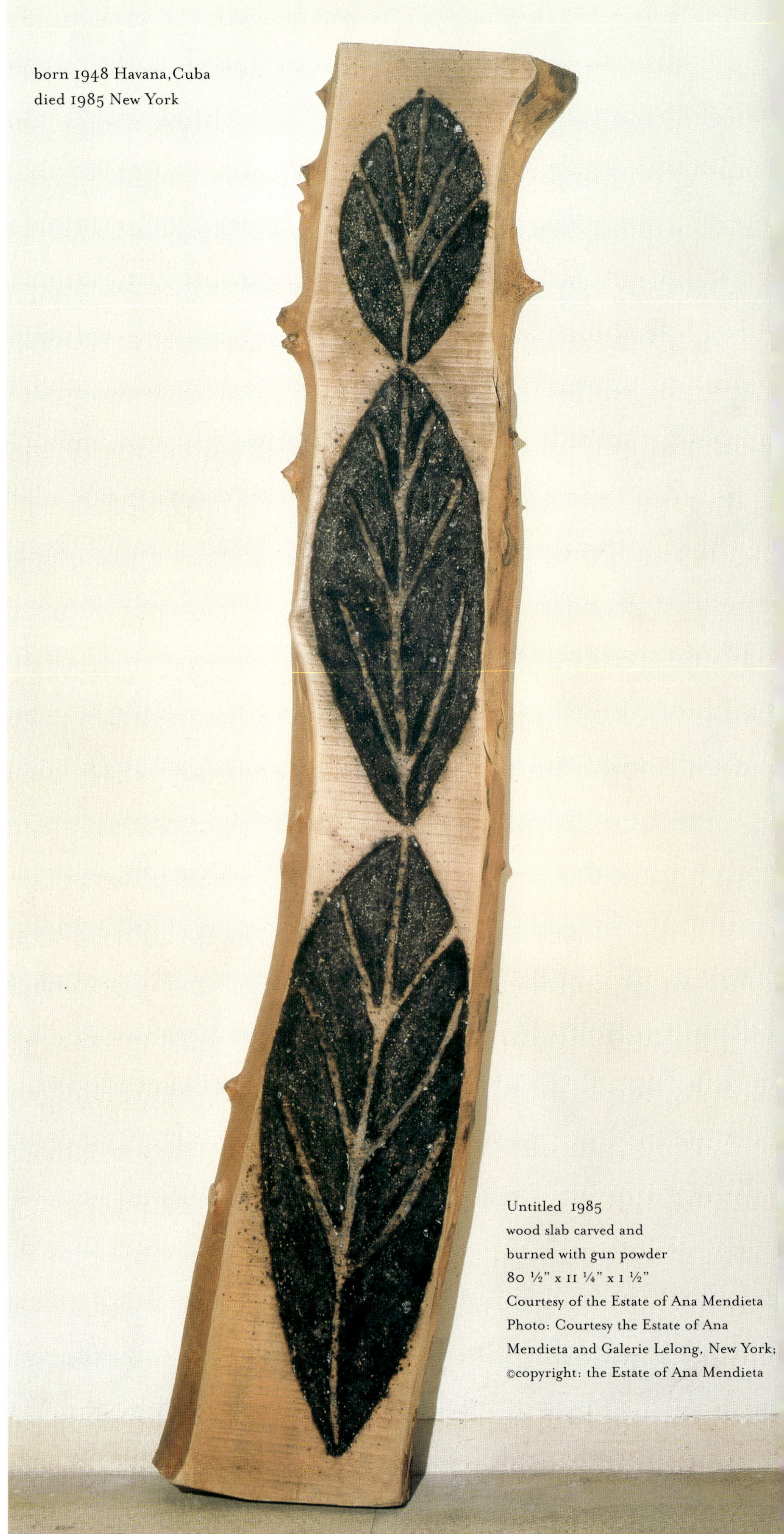

born 1948 Havana, Cuba
died 1985 New York

Untitled 1985
wood slab carved and
burned with gun powder
80 ½" x 11 ¼" x 1 ½"
Courtesy of the Estate of Ana Mendieta
Photo: Courtesy the Estate of Ana
Mendieta and Galerie Lelong, New York;
©copyright: the Estate of Ana Mendieta

born 1940 Chicago, Illinois

ELIZABETH MURRAY

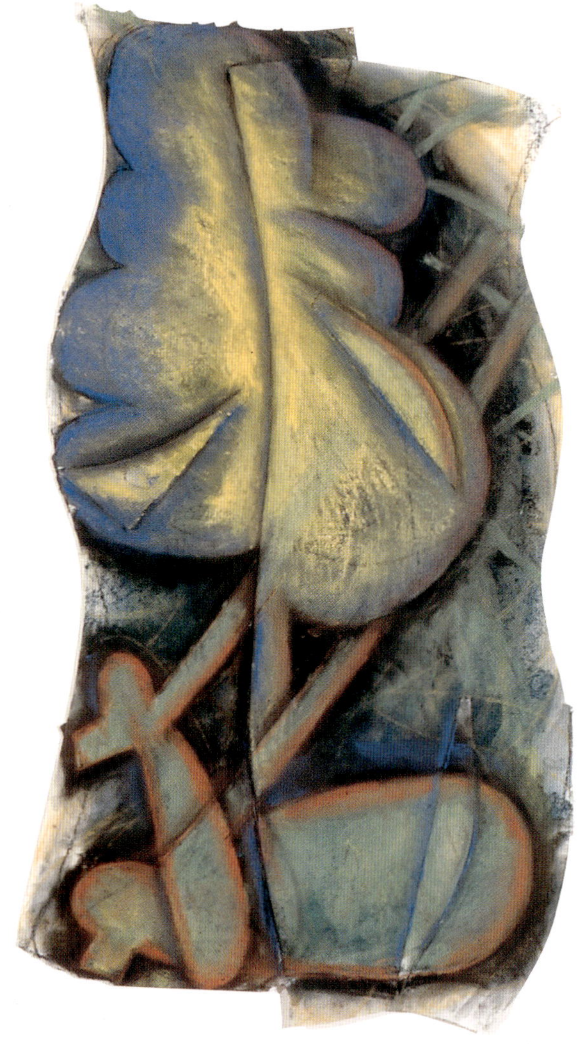

"I was living on White Street in 1976/77 and a guy gave me a box of really cheap pastels for Dakota (my son). They were sitting in my studio unused for a long time. Then one day I put up paper and I started to draw. I liked the feel of them, the softness, the mushiness. And then I really started. If I thought about pastels, I thought about Degas. I never thought about them for me…One thing led to another…" December 4, 1998

Stroll - 2 1986
pastel on 2 sheets of paper
46" x 24 ½"
Collection of Robert Lehrman, Washington, DC

"With wood sculpture one tends to see 'wood,' a warm, familiar material, before reading the form: wood first, form second. Charring radically changes this experience. The surface is transformed from a vegetable material to a mineral – carbon – and one sees the form before the material. The sense of scale and time are strangely changed, the charred form feels compacted yet distanced in an expanded space." David Nash in Llandudno, North Wales, 1990. from *David Nash Forms Into Time*, Academy Group Ltd., London (©1996).

born 1945 Esher, Surrey, England

DAVID NASH

Enfolded Space 1998
oak with charred interior
92 ½" x 29 ½" x 39"
Courtesy the artist and Galerie Lelong, New York

RIVANE NEUENSCHWANDER

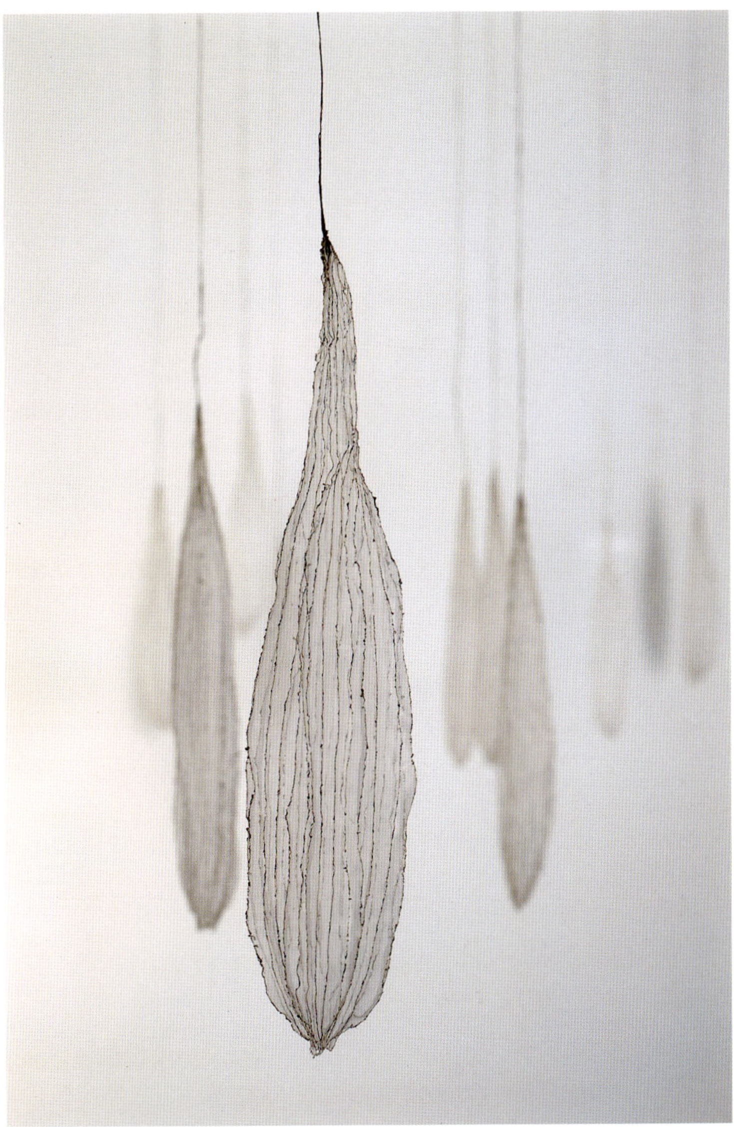

Untitled 1997
nylon burnt with incense, and vegetal hair
15" x 8" x 8" each
installation dimensions vary
Courtesy the artist and
Stephen Friedman Gallery, London

"I've been working with the reconstruction of fragments through obsessive waves of repetition, trying to respect the autonomous system from each material — a way I found to reveal their forgotten potential…I like to think about the transformation of things until they turn into powder and the obvious connotation it has related to death. Then I think about the "little deaths" which assault us daily and are not perceived, the small transformations which once added, can define — even being invisible — the course of our lives…About the incense, what interests me is the trace left by the fire (life) on the surface of things, even before it turns into powder (death). I like the ambiguity found in the action of using something related to 'protection' in order to modify the skin of things — to destroy and recreate at the same time." In correspondence with the artist, December 15, 1998.

CORNELIA PARKER

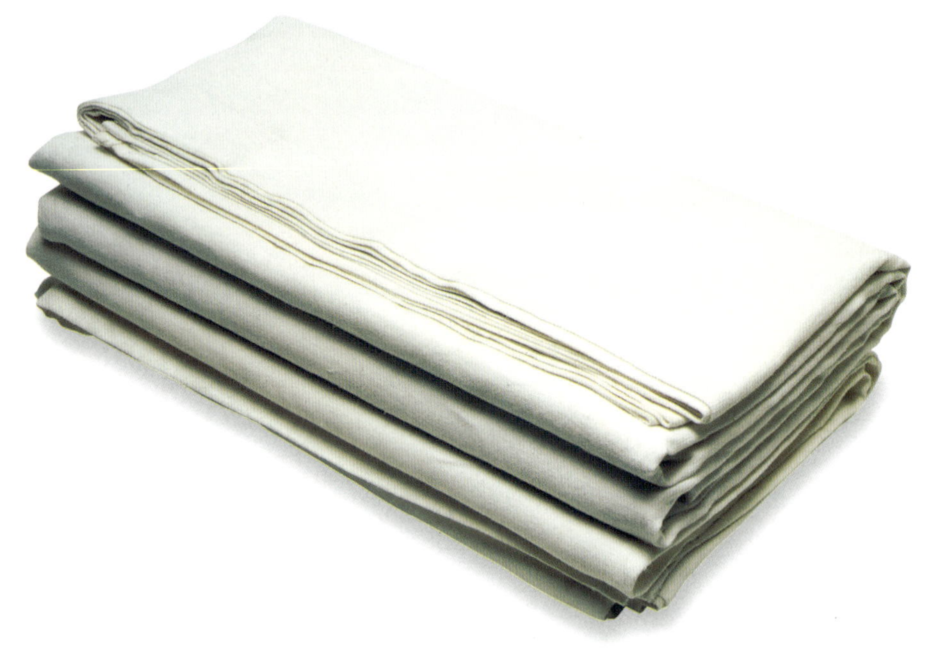

Inhaled Cliffs 1996
cotton sheets starched with chalk from
White Cliffs of Dover
25½" x 41" x 11"
Courtesy the artist and
Frith Street Gallery, London

born 1903 Dvinsk, Russia died 1970 New York

MARK ROTHKO

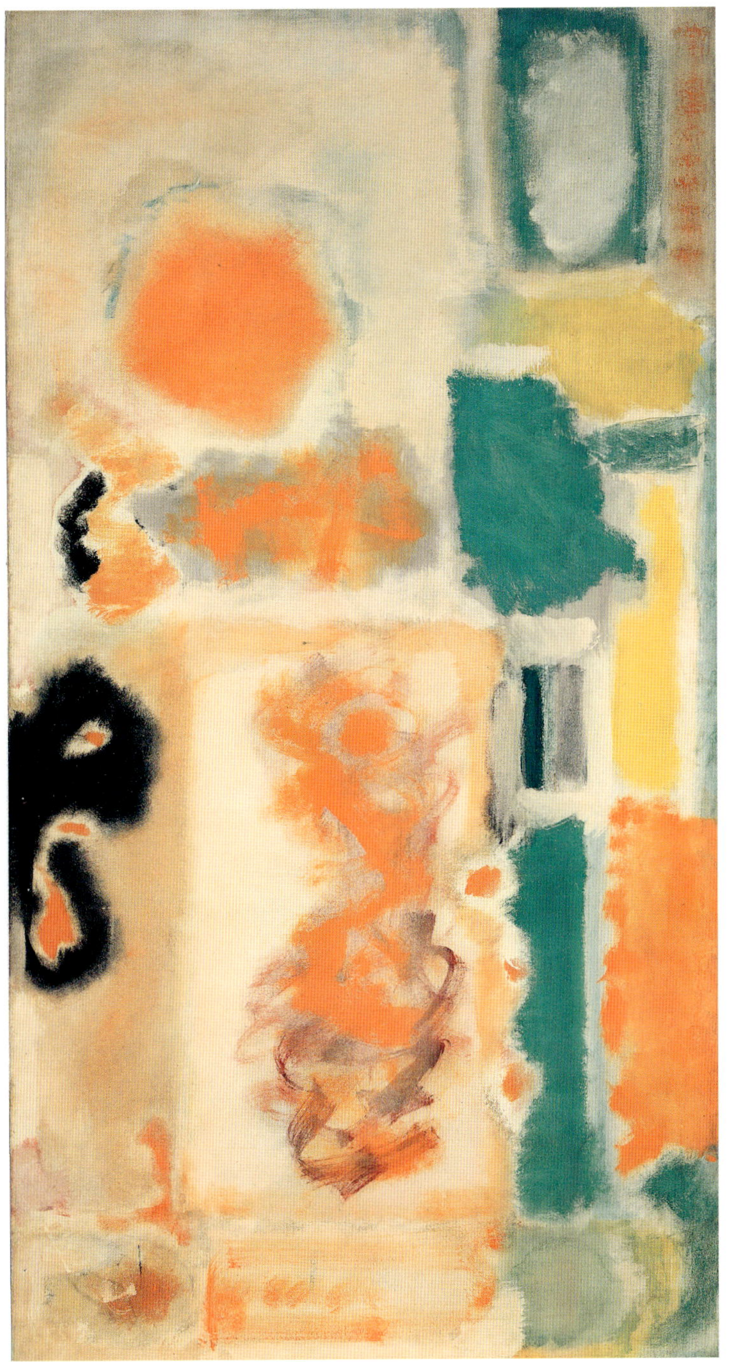

Untitled 1948
oil on canvas
62" x 32⅛"
Estate Number: 3019.38
Catalogue Raisonne Number: 384
Collection of Christopher Rothko
Artwork by Mark Rothko,
Copyright ©1998 by Christopher Rothko
and Kate Rothko Prizel

"I adhere to the material reality of the world and the substance of things."
In a personal statement by Mark Rothko for the exhibition, *A Painting Prophet: 1950,*
at the David Porter Gallery, Washington, DC. (February 3–28, 1945) as cited in the essay by
Gage, John. *Rothko: Color as Subject,* in *Mark Rothko,* National Gallery of Art, Washington,
Yale University Press (1998). p. 254.

born 1952 Naples, Texas

NANCY RUBINS

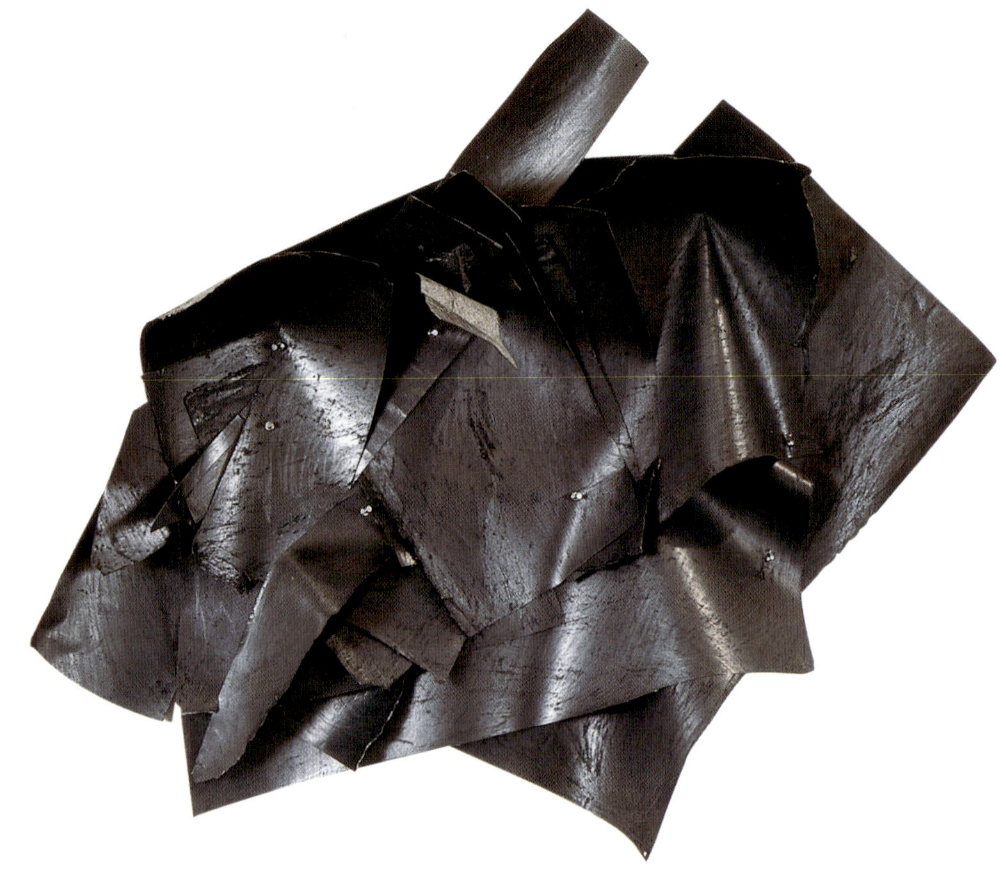

Drawings 1994
graphite on paper
43" x 37" x 12"
Courtesy the artist and
Paul Kasmin Gallery, New York

born 1937 Omaha, Nebraska

Edward Ruscha

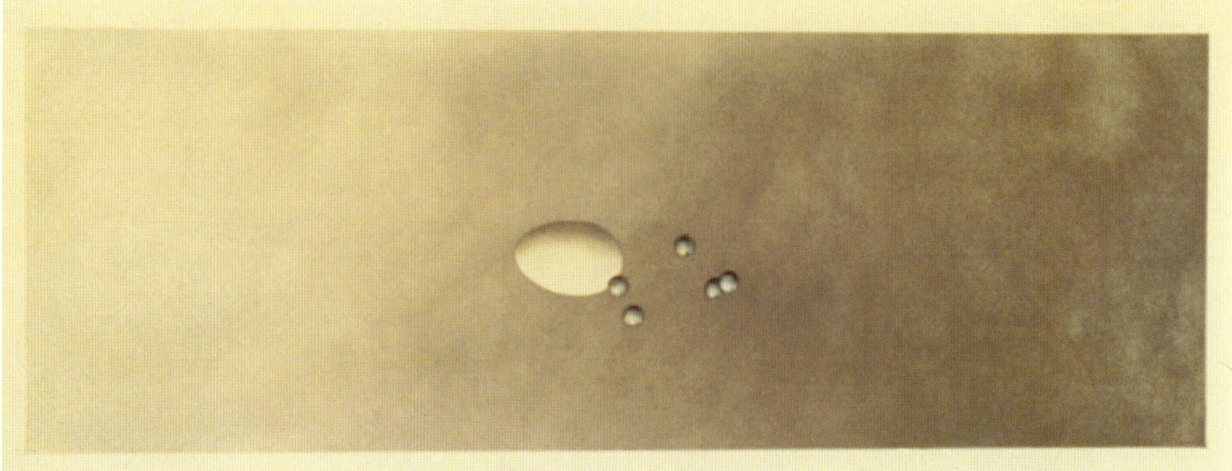

Whiskers, Splinters 1972
gunpowder and pastel
11½" x 29"
Collection Mr. and Mrs. James R. Hedges IV
Courtesy Thea Westreich Art Advisory Services

Ball Bearings 1971
gunpowder and pastel
11½" x 29"
Collection Mr. and Mrs. James R. Hedges IV
Courtesy Thea Westreich Art Advisory Services

"The use of gunpowder was accidental. It happened that a can of gunpowder granules was on a shelf with other art materials, mostly powders. The thought of using this was spontaneous. I had to soak the powder in water to wash out the salt to be compatible with drawing on paper. Before using it, I had worked almost exclusively with powdered lead from pencils and the effect was very good but any flaws were hard to correct. Gunpowder has a unique color, that of sulphur and charcoal, and the doctoring of any flaws was a simple thing." December 7, 1998.

ANTONI TAPIÈS

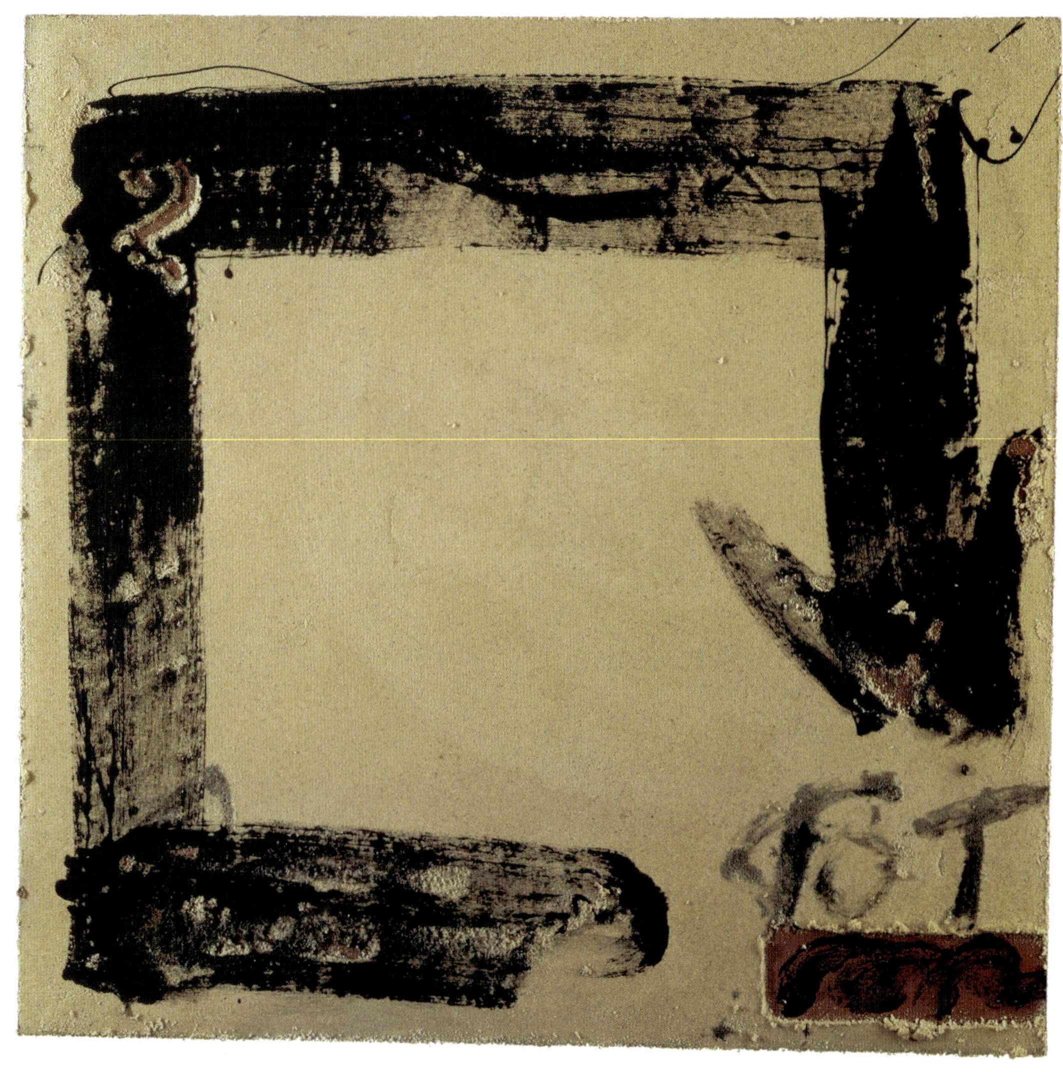

Quadrat 1995
marble dust and paint on wood
$39\frac{1}{2}$" x $39\frac{1}{2}$"
Courtesy PaceWildenstein Gallery, New York
Photo: Sarah Harper Gifford

born 1954 Santander, Spain

JUAN USLÉ

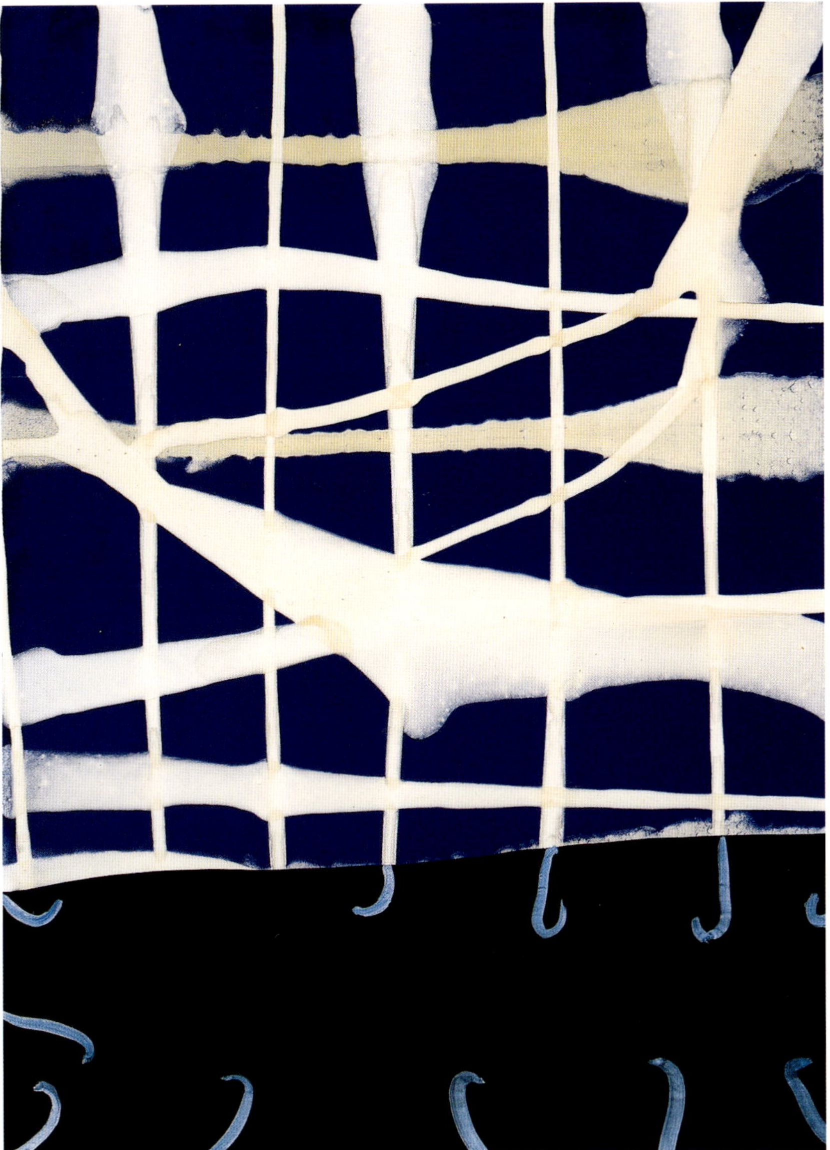

Cruzados 1994
dispersion vinyl and pigment on canvas
22" x 16"
Private Collection

"I began to use powder because paint was expensive for me to buy. So I decided to make my own paint, and in that process I soon became seduced by the special quality of light that dry pigment generates. The use of dry pigment helps my work to embody two components that are important to me in the process of visual perception: (1) the sense of reality, from the earthy presence of the material; and (2) the ability of the powder to keep alive an enigmatical illusion. Looking as perceiving a magical light. The reflection of light on dry pigment confers to the paintings also a unique sense of fragility." December 9, 1998.

ANDY WARHOL

Shadow circa 1979
synthetic polymer paint, diamond dust and silkscreen ink on canvas
76" x 52"
©1999 Andy Warhol Foundation for the Visual Arts, Inc./ARS, New York/Art Resource, NY

"I'd prefer to remain a mystery. I never like to give my background and, anyway, I make it all different every time I am asked."
Andy Warhol, quoted in Gretchen Berg, "Andy Warhol: My True Story," *Los Angeles Free Press* (March 1967). p. 42.

born 1944 San Francisco, California

MEG WEBSTER

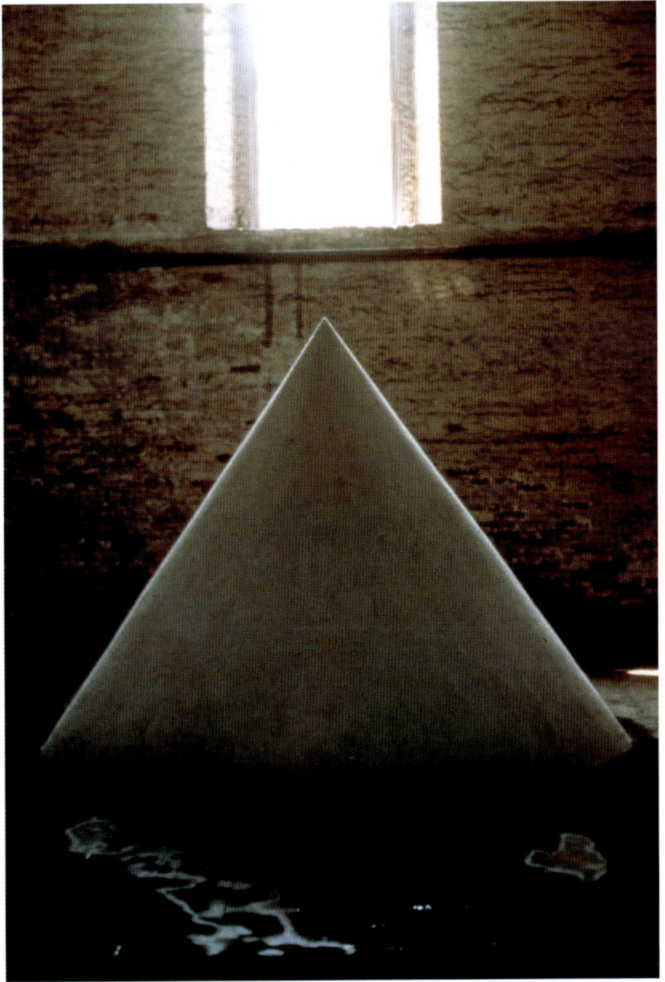

Cono di Sale 1988
7½' x 8'
Courtesy of the artist
Cono di Sale *is now destroyed.*
It was a cone of packed salt exhibited in an
installation at the XLIII Biennale di Venezia.
For POWDER, *the artist will create an*
outdoor sculpture of packed snow.

"In the beginning, working with sand, it became magical because I could make precise contoured forms that were both geometric and organic. There was a kind of 'hush' about them; one would sense that gravity was at work."
November 23, 1998.

born 1941 St. John's, Newfoundland, Canada

JACKIE WINSOR

"Choices of materials are odd in how they work their way into your life. When I first used colored pigments, the pigment was as weak as chalk and it was supported by other structures in my sculpture. Pigment colors are chemically active but when you put them together with other chemically active materials you gain knowledge of the chemistry of the joined material. When you push it, you are pushing the chemical properties and often they come to an unusual conclusion. It gets to be an oblique metaphor for finding yourself." December 6, 1998.

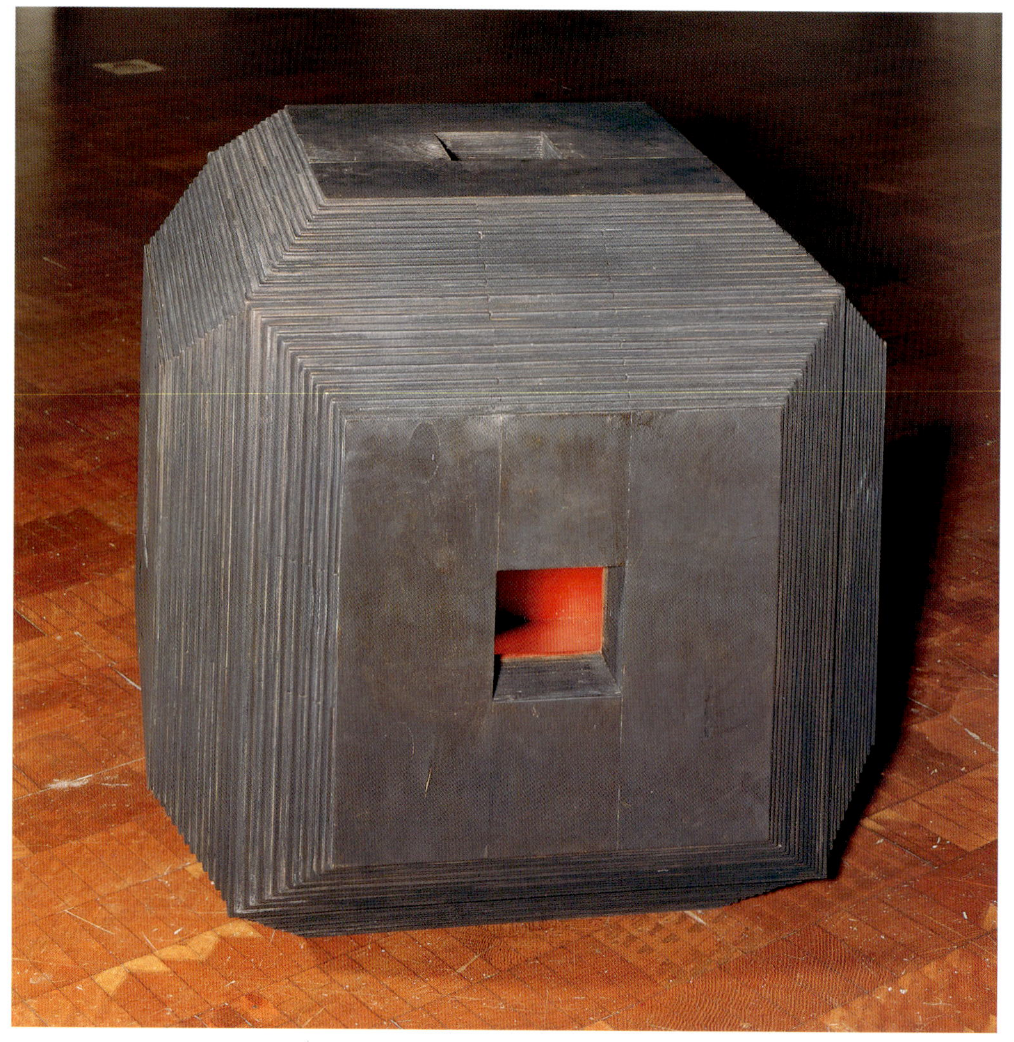

Burned and Red Inside-Out Piece 1985
plywood, plaster and pigment
30" x 30" x 30"
Collection of Martin Sklar, New York
Photo: Geoffrey Clements

born 1959 Fukuoka, Japan

YUKINORI YANAGI

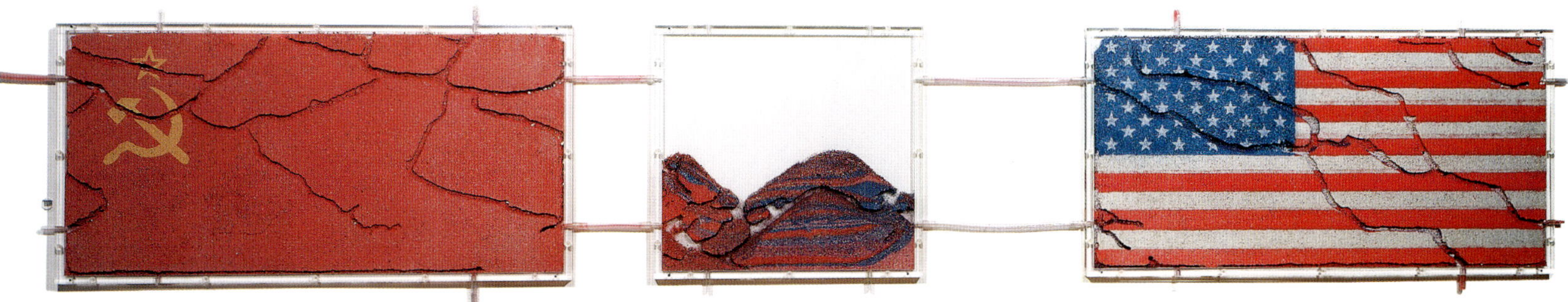

USA and USSR 1993
colored sand, Plexiglas boxes
two boxes: 16¾" x 32½" each;
one box: 16¾" x 17¾";
total length: 6' 10"
Nancy and Bob Magoon Collection
Photo: Hal Williams Photography

"At present my work looks toward a simple, equal, and hopeful way of expressing the world's gradual unification of all its nations…"
Yukinoro Yanagi in an artist's statement written for World Flag Art Farm (1990), reprinted from "Aperto: Yukinori Yanagi," Flash Art (Summer 1993), p. 95.

DAISY YOUNGBLOOD

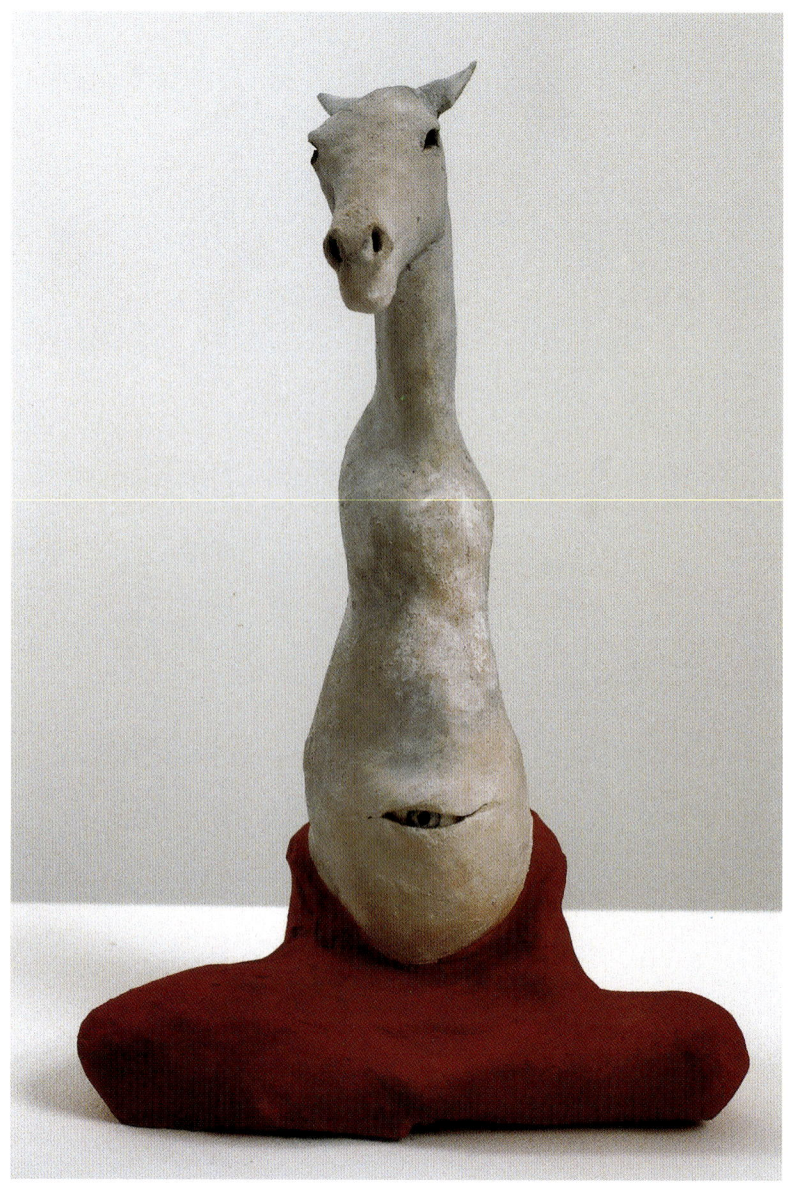

Sitting Horse 1996
low-fire clay & pigment
12¾" x 7½" x 4½"
Collection Gary and JoAnn Fink

JENNIFER BARTLETT
Homan-J; Series II, V-6   1992
Japanese mineral color on
handmade Kozo paper
25⅛" x 25⅛"
Collection Peggy and Dick Danziger,
New York

VIJA CELMINS
Untitled #10   1994-95
charcoal on paper
17⅛" x 22⅛"
Collection of David and Renee
McKee, New York

JOSEPH CORNELL
Untitled (Blue Sand Fountain)
circa 1960
mixed media box construction
11½" x 8" x 4"
Private collection
Courtesy Allan Stone Gallery,
New York

MARY CORSE
White Light Painting
(from the Bevel Series)   1994
micro-glass spheres in paint
on canvas
48" x 48"
Courtesy Ace Gallery, New York

JEAN DUBUFFET
Bouche en croissant ou Rieuse
à bouche en croissant de lune
(Crescent Mouth, or
Laughing Woman with a
Crescent-Moon Mouth)   1946
oil, pebbles and sand on canvas
25⅝" x 21¼"
National Gallery of Art, Washington
The Stephen Hahn Family Collection
(Partial and Promised Gift)

KATHARINA FRITSCH
Rattenkönig (Rat-King)   1998
polyester and paint; edition of eight
5⅞" x 23⅝" diameter
Courtesy Matthew Marks Gallery,
New York
©1999 Artists Rights Society (ARS),
New York/VG Bild-Kunst, Bonn

ANDY GOLDSWORTHY
Filled in under the branch arch with
snow made a hole that changed the
light (2/8/96)
photography, total nine images
31½" x 63¾" large photo
Collection Zoe and Joel Dictrow,
New York
Courtesy Galerie Lelong, New York

REBECCA HORN
Nightwood – Djuna Barnes   1990
motor, sieve, hammer,
face powder, book, steel
139½" x 12" x 12"
Courtesy Marian Goodman Gallery,
New York

RONI HORN
Untitled   1985
powdered pigment, varnish on paper
mounted on board
4⅝" x 6"
Collection Amy and Richard Lipton

Untitled   1985
powdered pigment, varnish on paper
mounted on board
7¼" x 6¼"
Collection Amy and Richard Lipton

ANISH KAPOOR
From 1000 Names…   1979-1980
wood, plaster, pigment
24" x 58" x 24"
Courtesy Barbara Gladstone Gallery,
New York

WILLIAM KENTRIDGE
Weighing and Wanting
image 9'10½" x 6'6¾"
room size 19'8" x 13'1½"
videotape
Courtesy Marian Goodman Gallery,
New York

YVES KLEIN
Sponge (Blue Sculpture)   1960
blue painted sponge and metal;
brass pedestal
6" x 8" x 6¾"
Nancy and Bob Magoon Collection

KOO JEONG-A
Oslo   1997
aspirin
4" x 36" x 30"
Courtesy the artist and
Barbara Gladstone Gallery, New York

WOLFGANG LAIB
Untitled   1998
hazelnut pollen
2¾" high
Courtesy Sperone Westwater Gallery,
New York

JULIAN LETHBRIDGE
Untitled   1994-95
oil, graphite on linen
20⅛" x 16"
Courtesy the artist and
Paula Cooper Gallery, New York

MAYA LIN
Untitled (Crater Series)   1998
beeswax and glass beads
9" x 7" x 1½"
Courtesy the artist and
Gagosian Gallery, New York

RICHARD LONG
Untitled   1991
Mississippi mud on paper
78" x 43⅛"
Chase Manhattan Collection

SUZANNE McCLELLAND
First   1998
absorbent ground, enamel,
polymer emulsion, acrylic, charcoal,
dry pigment and conte on canvas
48" x 40"
Courtesy Weaver Collection,
Michigan

ANA MENDIETA
Untitled   1985
wood slab carved and
burned with gun powder
80 ½" x 11 ¼" x 1 ½"
Courtesy of the Estate of
Ana Mendieta
Copyright: the Estate of Ana Mendieta

ELIZABETH MURRAY
Stroll - 2   1986
pastel on 2 sheets of paper
46" x 24 ½"
Collection of Robert Lehrman,
Washington, DC

DAVID NASH
Enfolded Space   1998
oak with charred interior
92 ½" x 29 ½" x 39"
Courtesy the artist and
Galerie Lelong, New York

RIVANE NEUENSCHWANDER
Untitled   1997
nylon burnt with incense,
and vegetal hair
15" x 8" x 8" each
installation dimensions vary
Courtesy the artist and
Stephen Friedman Gallery, London

CORNELIA PARKER
Inhaled Cliffs   1996
cotton sheets starched with chalk
from White Cliffs of Dover
25½" x 41" x 11"
Courtesy the artist and
Frith Street Gallery, London

MARK ROTHKO
Untitled   1948
oil on canvas
62" x 32⅛"
Estate Number: 3019.38
Catalogue Raisonne Number: 384
Collection of Christopher Rothko
Artwork by Mark Rothko, Copyright
©1998 by Christopher Rothko and
Kate Rothko Prizel

NANCY RUBINS
Drawings   1994
graphite on paper
43" x 37" x 12"
Courtesy the artist and
Paul Kasmin Gallery, New York

EDWARD RUSCHA
Ball Bearings   1971
gunpowder and pastel
11½" x 29"
Collection of Mr. and Mrs. James R.
Hedges IV
Courtesy Thea Westreich Art
Advisory Services

Whiskers, Splinters   1972
gunpowder and pastel
11½" x 29"
Collection of Mr. and Mrs. James R.
Hedges IV
Courtesy Thea Westreich Art
Advisory Services

ANTONI TAPIÈS
Quadrat   1995
marble dust and paint on wood
39½" x 39½"
Courtesy PaceWildenstein Gallery,
New York

JUAN USLÉ
Cruzados   1994
dispersion vinyl and pigment on canvas
22" x 16"
Private collection

ANDY WARHOL
Shadow   circa 1979
synthetic polymer paint, diamond
dust and silkscreen ink on canvas
76" x 52"
Andy Warhol Foundation for the
Visual Arts, Inc./ARS, New York/
Art Resource, NY

MEG WEBSTER
For POWDER, the artist will create
an outdoor sculpture of packed snow.

JACKIE WINSOR
Burned and Red Inside-Out Piece
1985
plywood, plaster and pigment
30" x 30" x 30"
Collection of Martin Sklar,
New York

YUKINORI YANAGI
USA and USSR   1993
colored sand, Plexiglas boxes
two boxes: 16¾" x 32½" each;
one box: 16¾" x 17¾"
total length: 6' 10"
Nancy and Bob Magoon Collection

DAISY YOUNGBLOOD
Sitting Horse   1996
low-fire clay & pigment
12¾" x 7½" x 4½"
Collection Gary and JoAnn Fink

ABOUT THE COVER: Flocking is a process in which
powdered wool is scattered onto paper and adhered with
glue or slow-drying varnish. Red was chosen because of
the origin and systemic meanings of the word itself, and
because of its organic sources and associations. The
Proto-Indo-European family of languages is among the
largest in the world, and a version of the Proto-Indo-
European *reudh (red)*, including the German *rot* and the
Latin *rufus*, appears in them all. The name for the first
human being, the first man, is *Adam*. He is so named
because he is "made of earth" *Adamah* (earth in Hebrew)
and guardian of the earth. The color red is from the
same root, *Adom* — the connection between man and earth.
In nature, red is the color of blood, fire, clay, various
flowers and ripe fruits. It is the rust in grain, the color
in magma, the mineral rich lava from earth's center.
It is the color of joyful occurences and the root dye from
East Indian woods. The color of vitality, of memory
and mortality. It is a symbol for "vital presence," a state
of being that chooses to act, that is IN THE PRESENT.